ILTS

Speech-Language Pathologist: Nonteaching (154) Practice Questions

Mometrix
TEST PREPARATION

Dear Future Exam Success Story

First of all, **THANK YOU** for purchasing Mometrix study materials!

Second, congratulations! You are one of the few determined test-takers who are committed to doing whatever it takes to excel on your exam. **You have come to the right place.** We developed these practice tests with one goal in mind: to deliver you the best possible approximation of the questions you will see on test day.

Standardized testing is one of the biggest obstacles on your road to success, which only increases the importance of doing well in the high-pressure, high-stakes environment of test day. Your results on this test could have a significant impact on your future, and these practice tests will give you the repetitions you need to build your familiarity and confidence with the test content and format to help you achieve your full potential on test day.

Your success is our success

We would love to hear from you! If you would like to share the story of your exam success or if you have any questions or comments in regard to our products, please contact us at **800-673-8175** or **support@mometrix.com**.

Thanks again for your business and we wish you continued success!

Sincerely,
The Mometrix Test Preparation Team

Printed in the United States of America

Table of Contents

Practice Test #1

1. ASHA recommends that all children receive hearing screenings at what age?

a. From 3 to 6 years
b. 12 to 18 months
c. 3 to 6 months
d. Birth

2. What is/are the primary *sensory* part(s) of the hearing mechanism?

a. Auricle/pinna
b. Auditory meatus
c. Tympanic membrane
d. Cochlea and Organ of Corti

3. Children with Down syndrome often have some articulatory distortion, particularly with consonants like /s/. What is this due to primarily?

a. Mental characteristics
b. Physical characteristics
c. Behavioral characteristics
d. Unknown sources

4. Donna is a speech therapist who has just moved to a new school. She inherits a caseload from the previous person who was not a speech therapist but a general education teacher with some course credits in special education. She discovers that one student, Erin, has been placed in a special education classroom with other "speech therapy students." However, the other students in this group all have delayed language development, whereas Erin stutters. Erin reads and writes above grade level, has a high IQ score and a large vocabulary, and gets good grades in all subjects. What action should Donna take?

a. Keep Erin in the same group but also does a lot of one-on-one stuttering therapy with her.
b. Find two other students who stutter and form a new group with them and Erin.
c. Advocate for Erin to be in the general classroom with speech therapy sessions.
d. Work individually with Erin, as her stutter would humiliate her in the classroom.

5. A patient is diagnosed with dysphagia, but testing is required to determine its cause. Of the following tests, which one measures the patient's esophageal pressure during swallowing?

a. Manometry
b. Laryngoscopy
c. pH monitoring
d. Esophagoscopy

6. Of the following congenital syndromes that can cause speech-language problems, which one is classified as a chromosomal syndrome?

a. Hurler syndrome
b. Hunter syndrome
c. Turner syndrome
d. Phenylketonuria

7. Which of the following adults would be the best candidate for cochlear implants?

a. One who hears very well using hearing aids
b. One with moderate unilateral hearing loss
c. One who strongly embraces deaf culture
d. One who lost his or her hearing in adolescence

8. What does recruitment mean in audiology?

a. Reduced range between threshold, MCL, and UCL
b. Recruiting other nerves to supplant damaged nerves
c. Recruiting hearing acuity for barely audible sounds
d. Abnormally wide range between threshold and MCL

9. Which of the following is included among direct methods of stuttering therapy?

a. Changing a stutterer's environment
b. Modifying parents' speech patterns
c. Focusing on the stutterer's feelings
d. Increasing pauses in conversations

10. Of the following impairments in airway protection related to swallowing, which is MOST likely to cause aspiration *during* swallowing rather than before or after swallowing?

a. Liquids entering the pharynx too soon due to poor oral containment
b. Delayed laryngeal closure after a bolus is propelled into the pharynx
c. Poor vocal fold closure from paralysis, weakness, or anatomical fixation
d. Residual material accumulated in the pharynx and not all swallowed

11. What do people diagnosed with Broca's aphasia have more difficulty with?

a. Comprehending questions others ask them
b. Understanding statements made by others
c. Discriminating among heard speech sounds
d. Asking questions and/or making statements.

12. Of the following examples of phonological processes (= developmentally normal, predictable pronunciation errors typically made by young children still learning correct speech), which has the *youngest* age norm for its elimination?

a. Pronouncing "fish" as "tish"
b. Pronouncing "very" as "berry"
c. Pronouncing "juice" as "deuce"
d. Pronouncing "thing" as "ting"

13. Alison is a fourth-grade student with a speech-language impairment due to stuttering. Which of the following strategies would be least effective in providing a supportive classroom environment?

a. Having her use prerecorded audio for presentations in which she has to speak
b. Having her collaborate with students that she is comfortable with
c. Having the teacher refrain from calling on her in class
d. Having her sit near the teacher at the front of class

14. Of the following cranial nerves, which has explicitly motor functions?

a. V
b. III
c. X
d. IX

15. You are an SLP in a public elementary school. A group of African-American children are referred to you to evaluate for services to remediate delayed language development. They all use expressions like "She happy" and "There go Bobby." What are these evidence of?

a. A common speech disorder
b. A shared language disorder
c. A regional dialect's usages
d. A cultural dialect's usages

16. Which statement is most accurate regarding the role of counseling in an SLP's work?

a. For SLPs, providing counseling consists of giving information, instruction, and advice.
b. SLP clinicians can increase the effectiveness of their other treatments via counseling.
c. SLPs who provide counseling take the place of psychologists or professional counselors.
d. Counseling by SLPs does not address the emotional impact of the client's impairment.

17. Which of the following describes the purpose of an intelligence test?

a. To measure a student's ability to think abstractly
b. To measure a student's ability to understand spoken language
c. To measure a student's ability to convey ideas through oral language
d. To measure a student's ability to retain visual information

18. On which of the following does learning theory focus?

a. Unconscious impulses
b. Internal mechanisms
c. Social relationships
d. Observable behaviors

19. If a child is able to form words correctly but unable to string them together correctly to form a sentence, the child's issue is with:

a. Morphology
b. Syntax
c. Semantics
d. Memory

20. Which of the following reinforcement types has the highest resistance to extinction?

a. Variable-ratio
b. Variable-interval
c. Fixed-ratio
d. Fixed-interval

21. Which statement is MOST accurate about the context of treatment for language disorders?

a. Early interventions for young children not yet attending school should be in a clinical setting.
b. For older children identified with disorders, by law, treatment should only be given in school.
c. Treatment should be given in as many settings as possible including home, school, and clinic.
d. In schools, integrating language goals in the classroom should progress to pull-out programs.

22. "When reading aloud, John will raise his hand to signal 90% of his stuttering occurrences without cueing." This is an example of a behavioral objective for:

a. Speech awareness
b. Speech description
c. Speech modification
d. Speech preparation

23. Which of the following MOST refutes an argument for neurological causes of stuttering?

a. Research has found that more boys than girls exhibit dysfluencies.
b. Children over 6 years old can demonstrate persistent dysfluencies.
c. Stuttering is found to occur more commonly in twins than others.
d. Stuttering has been found to occur more often in the left-handed.

24. Models of behavior modification typically use which of the following to effect changes?

a. What the individual is thinking
b. What the individual is sensing
c. What the individual is feeling
d. What the individual is doing

25. An individual's audiogram shows a level of 10 dB in the left ear at 500 Hz; 60 dB in the right ear at 500 Hz; 50 dB in the left ear at 8000 Hz; and 90 dB in the right ear at 8000 Hz. How would this person's hearing loss be described?

a. Asymmetrical
b. Unilateral
c. Symmetrical
d. High-frequency

26. Of the following SLP activities for autistic children, which is MOST age-appropriate for an elementary school-aged child?

a. Reinforcing the child's responding to hearing his or her name
b. Practicing phrases and strategies for interacting with peers
c. Teaching the child to ask social questions of his or her peers
d. Practicing skills for successful responses in job interviews

27. Mendel first discovered by breeding pea plants that when the ________ for seed color is ________, the ________ reflects the _______ allele.

a. Phenotype; homozygous; genotype; recessive
b. Genotype; heterozygous; phenotype; dominant
c. Phenotype; heterozygous; genotype; recessive
d. Genotype; homozygous; phenotype; dominant

28. While the anatomy and physiology of speech production is more than the sum of its parts, for the sake of convenience the speech mechanism can be divided into four phases. Which of the following is NOT one of these?

a. Respiration
b. Phonation
c. Modulation
d. Articulation

29. Regarding the mandates of the IDEA and NCLB, which of these is true about increased accountability in designing assessments and treatments that comply with these laws?

a. Students with disabilities have always been assigned the same curricula as the nondisabled.
b. Academic performance standards for disabled students no longer mean grade-level content.
c. These laws both mandate the inclusion of disabled students in state and district assessments.
d. Using accommodations necessary to test and treat disabled students is not required by law.

30. According to ASHA's Code of Ethics, which of the following SLP behaviors regarding client prognoses would be ethical?

a. To tell clients and family it is impossible to give a prognosis because SLP is too complicated.
b. To give clients and family members some general idea about prognosis after evaluation.
c. To tell clients and family giving a prognosis is unethical by guaranteeing therapy results.
d. To give clients and family a prognosis only with standardized test results on the disorder.

31. Miles has recently come to America from his native England. He pronounces words like *thing, think, thank you,* and *other* as "fing," "fink," "fank you," and "uvver." What is the best explanation for this?

a. An articulation disorder
b. A phonological disorder
c. A language disorder
d. A regional dialect

32. If a child has a mild hearing loss between birth and 3 years of age, which of these is true?

a. If the loss is mild, the child's language skills are not harmed.
b. Language learning at this age does not need perfect hearing.
c. This will interfere with a critical period of language learning.
d. There is not enough research into mild hearing loss to know.

33. Elise is a fourth-grader who palatalizes her /tʃ/sound (i.e., her tongue is pressed up against her hard palate), noticeably distorting it. Glenda the SLP mentions this student to her predecessor Linda, who was Elise's SLP last year, and Linda affirms she was completely unsuccessful in remediating this articulation error. Glenda hits upon the idea of giving Elise a tongue depressor, instructing her to use it initially to keep her tongue from touching her palate while producing the target phoneme. Once Elise has become accustomed to the feeling of this tongue position and the sound she produces, Glenda has her phase out the tongue depressor until eventually she is pronouncing the sound correctly without it. Which of the following conclusions about this episode is most likely?

a. Elise's success this year is due to maturation alone and the treatment was superfluous.
b. Glenda's solution of the tongue depressor was entirely responsible for Elise's success.
c. Elise's success is most likely due to a combination of the therapy and her maturation.
d. Elise's success was due to her choice to change her speech, not therapy or maturation.

34. What is NOT a disadvantage of silicone prostheses inserted via the tracheoesophageal puncture (TEP) technique for a postoperative total laryngectomy patient?

a. Prosthesis maintenance
b. Time between replacement of the device
c. Low resistance to the flow of air
d. Total expense

35. According to reviews of the research literature, which of the following correctly represents a recent (post-2005) trend related to teacher referrals of students to school SLPs?

a. Teachers have been over-referring students for voice and articulation treatment.
b. Those reviewing the literature note the need for much more up-to-date research.
c. Teachers are highly aware of clinical concerns with socially withdrawn behaviors.
d. Those research studies of SLP services reviewed were all conducted in the 2000s.

36. Mary Ellen has diagnoses of both cerebral palsy and spastic dysarthria. What does spastic dysarthria indicate?

a. She cannot hear speech.
b. She cannot produce speech.
c. She cannot understand words.
d. She cannot sort speech sounds.

37. Hearing aids _______ sounds, whereas cochlear implants _______ sounds.

a. Convert; amplify
b. Amplify; convert
c. Transmit; sharpen
d. Sharpen; transmit

38. The parts of the body associated most closely with speech production obviously include the oral cavity, including the lips, tongue, and teeth. Which of the following is NOT one of the body parts *normally* most closely involved?

a. The larynx
b. The trachea
c. The esophagus
d. The nasal cavities

39. An effective and desirable voice prosthetic should include all of the following features EXCEPT?

a. Safe and reliable use
b. A loose-fitting fistula capable of expansion
c. Frontloading insertion
d. Semipermanent fixation

40. Which of the following etiologies of dysphagia is obstructive in nature?

a. Cleft palate
b. Edentulism
c. Xerostomia
d. Esophagitis

41. In acoustic phonetics, what is the greatest change from normal atmospheric air pressure?

a. Period
b. Frequency
c. Amplitude
d. Wavelength

42. Which of the following is accurate regarding provisions of the NCLB Act (2001)?

a. States but not individual schools are more accountable.
b. Local use of federal education funds has stricter rules.
c. Parents are to be more involved in children's education.
d. Federal, not state, standards qualify states for funding.

43. In which of the following practice settings is the SLP the one responsible for deciding when to terminate speech-language therapy?

a. In Birth-to-3 programs
b. In public school systems
c. In health care systems
d. In none of these

44. The confidentiality provisions of the IDEA include that every participating agency keep records of parties obtaining access to a child's education records including name, date, and purpose for which the party is authorized to use the records. What types of access does this include?

a. Access by the parents of the child of the records used
b. Access by any employees of the participating agency
c. Access by both the parents and agency employees
d. Access by neither parents nor agency employees

45. You would expect to use Melodic Intonation Therapy (MIT) for a client with which of the following diagnoses?

a. Transcortical sensory aphasia
b. Wernicke's aphasia
c. Broca's aphasia
d. Conduction aphasia

46. If a child consistently says "muh" every time he or she sees or is given milk, which of the following is true?

a. This is an example of nonreduplicated babbling.
b. This normally occurs around the age of 14 to 24 months.
c. This is a typical feature of the later one-word stage.
d. This is an example of vocalizations called protowords.

47. Which is the least common feature of functional dysphonias?

a. Breathy voice
b. Loud voice
c. Weak voice
d. Harsh voice

48. According to ASHA's treatment efficacy summaries, which of the following populations demonstrated the largest proportion of gain from SLP interventions?

a. Patients who had aphasia secondary to left-hemisphere strokes
b. Preschool children with diagnoses of autism spectrum disorders
c. Preschool-aged children identified as having language disorders
d. Dysphagic adults starting treatment at home with feeding tubes

49. Which of the following is an example of a descriptive research design?

a. A case study
b. A cohort study
c. A longitudinal study
d. A cross-sectional study

50. Which of the following malocclusions is *most* likely to cause distortion of sibilants?

a. Overbite
b. Open-bite
c. Underbite
d. Cross-bite

51. In human children, which of the following brain structures involved in language is the *latest* to complete its development?

a. Broca's area
b. Wernicke's area
c. The hippocampus
d. The prefrontal cortex

52. Which of the following is NOT a component of a lesson plan for speech-language therapy?

a. Goals for the semester
b. Behavioral objectives
c. Describing activities
d. Medical history

53. A 1-year-old typically can point using the forefinger. What is this MOST closely associated with?

a. Cognitive skills
b. Motor skills
c. Sensory skills
d. Language skills

54. Which is accurate about people sustaining damage to the left hemispheres of their brains?

a. The majority of left-handed people with this damage will have aphasia.
b. Roughly half of right-handed people with this damage will have aphasia.
c. The majority of right-handed people with this damage will have aphasia.
d. Handedness regardless, most people with this damage will have aphasia.

55. With enough training and practice, which form of alaryngeal speech is found to be clearest?

a. Buccal speech
b. Pharyngeal speech
c. Esophageal speech
d. None of these

56. What kind of language do patients who are diagnosed with Broca's aphasia have more problems with?

a. Receptive
b. Academic
c. Everyday
d. Expressive

57. Which of these concern(s) the patterns, systems, and rules of speech sounds in a language?

a. Phonology
b. Phonetics
c. Phonemics
d. All of these

58. Which of the following is correct regarding velopharyngeal mislearning?

a. Velopharyngeal mislearning is a phenomenon unrelated to hearing loss.
b. Velopharyngeal mislearning causes phoneme-specific nasal air emission.
c. Velopharyngeal mislearning primarily causes hyponasality of the speech.
d. Velopharyngeal mislearning is treated by speech therapy and/or surgery.

59. What does the stapedius reflex do?

a. Amplifies sound waves for hearing
b. Activates the stapes so it vibrates
c. Protects the ears from loud noises
d. Enables us to hear our own voices

60. For individuals with intellectual disabilities receiving SLP services, which of the following is the MOST recent or current practice for determining when to discharge the client?

a. When a plateau has been encountered in the effects of the treatment
b. When client communication status matches his or her cognitive level
c. When the client applies learned functional skills in everyday routines
d. When the client feels that the effects of the treatment are complete

61. Which of these statements is NOT true of stuttering?

a. Boys are twice as likely to stutter as girls are.
b. As they age, fewer boys are likely to stutter.
c. The majority of children outgrow stuttering.
d. Around 1% or fewer of adults are stutterers.

62. Which neuromuscular activities does the normal adult human processes of eating and swallowing involve?

a. Both
b. Neither
c. Voluntary
d. Involuntary

63. Two- to three-year-old children normally develop the ability to understand and ask "Why" questions. Which domain of language is this an example of?

a. Phonology
b. Semantics
c. Syntax
d. Pragmatics

64. Of the following evaluation procedures defined under Part C of the IDEA, which reflects the need to establish the student's present speech-language status?

a. The SLP administers an evaluation instrument to the student.
b. The SLP interviews the parents and obtains the child's history.
c. The SLP obtains student information from various informants.
d. The SLP reviews the student's medical and education records.

65. Which of the following cranial nerves is NOT necessary for speech?

a. V
b. VII
c. XI
d. XII

66. Susan is 7 years old. While her articulation was previously normal, this year, when asked her name and age, she says, "Thuthan" and "Theven." What is the MOST common and likely reason for this change?

a. She has a developmental disorder.
b. She has lost her upper front teeth.
c. She has not reached the age norm.
d. She has just suffered hearing loss.

67. Which of the following is correct regarding progressive motor neuron diseases?

a. Progressive Bulbar Palsy (PBP) involves the degeneration of only the upper motor neurons.
b. Spinal Muscular Atrophy (SMA) causes the deterioration of both the upper and the lower motor neurons.
c. Primary Lateral Sclerosis (PLS) involves the deterioration of only the lower motor neurons.
d. Amyotrophic Lateral Sclerosis (ALS) includes degeneration of both upper and lower motor neurons.

68. To adhere to the principles of test construction, what is true about what the manual for a standardized test should include?

a. There is no need for the authors to offer their rationale for the test.
b. Which qualifications are required of examiners should be identified.
c. Making a description of how the test was developed is unnecessary.
d. Only administering, scoring, and interpreting directions are needed.

69. When contrasting the stuttering therapy techniques of fluency shaping versus stuttering modification, which of the following is a characteristic of fluency shaping?

a. Desensitizing the client from aversive feelings about stuttering
b. Decreasing the stutterer's anxiety and avoidance behaviors
c. Increasing the complexity of utterances via incremental steps
d. Increasing the stutterer's self-confidence and sense of worth

70. Which of the following is NOT one of the seven subscales measured by the Adolescent Language Screening Test (ALST)?

a. Expressive vocabulary
b. Pragmatics
c. Rate
d. Phonology

71. For an incoming student from a different culture, which of the following characteristics has the greatest impact on the identification of special education needs?

a. The language the student speaks
b. The content the student has learned
c. The location the student comes from
d. The religion the student practices

72. Cleft palate is known to cause hypernasality. Among other organic etiologies, which does NOT cause a hypernasal voice?

a. An elongated palate
b. Surgical trauma
c. Soft palate injury
d. Neurological impairment

73. What kind of disorder does a patient diagnosed with Wernicke's aphasia predominantly have?

a. Expressive
b. Mixed
c. Receptive
d. Articulation

74. During an SLP student's supervised Clinical Fellowship (CF), what is correct about Medicare's requirements for who signs the student's clinical reports?

a. In states licensing CFs, the supervising SLP must cosign these if he or she gave direct supervision.
b. In states not licensing CFs, the supervising SLP never has to sign or cosign such clinical reports.
c. In states licensing CFs, the supervising SLP must always sign reports as the qualified provider.
d. In states not licensing CFs, the supervising SLP only signs them if he or she gave direct supervision.

75. Which of these intervention formats would be least applicable to learning synonyms and antonyms?

a. Identification, differentiation, and elaboration of meaning
b. Semantic classification and categorization
c. Judgment of consistency of meaning
d. Lexical paraphrasing

76. Joseph has Down syndrome. He can communicate with short, simple verbal phrases. He can read only a few words that he learned over a long time. He lives just a few blocks from his school. His area is not served by the school bus system. His teacher has a goal for Joseph to learn the directions to and from school so his mother will no longer need to accompany him. Which of these would be a good way for the teacher to work with him on this goal?

a. Send Joseph out first with a map, monitoring him remotely.
b. Send Joseph out first with written directions and shadow him from a distance.
c. Walk with Joseph, prompting him to verbalize the route until he learns it.
d. Gradually decrease the number of days his mother walks with him

77. Of the following theorists of cognitive development, who stated that the requirements for learning are attention, retention, reproduction, and motivation?

a. Piaget
b. Bandura
c. Skinner
d. Vygotsky

78. Jason is a bright, happy, active four-year-old whose IQ scores are above average. He is healthy and his audiological testing is normal. His mother reports that 2-3 days after birth he was observed to have jaundice and lethargy, which resolved in an equally short time. These symptoms were recorded at the hospital but not diagnosed or treated as they resolved so quickly. Jason is referred to an SLP because his speech is fluent but characterized by substitution of glottal stops for many consonants, which he seems unable to produce by using the normal configurations of tongue, teeth, and shape of the oral cavity. The most likely reason for this is that:

a. Jason is simply lazy about using his mouth and is using his throat instead.
b. Jason's development is normal; his speech will correct without treatment.
c. Jason formed this habit in his early speech and did not grow out of it.
d. Jason probably sustained minimal neurological damage when a newborn.

79. Ms. Banus is certified in speech-language pathology and audiology. Which professional organization membership does she hold to facilitate her services to students, their families, and her colleagues?

a. AAIDD
b. ASHA
c. APA
d. CCBD

80. Tina's family came here from China. In school, Tina consistently drops the *–s* endings from plural nouns. What is this MOST due to?

a. Tina's lack of familiarity with English as a new language
b. The fact that Tina has an undiagnosed language disorder
c. An idiolectal variation present only in Tina's English use
d. Transfer from Tina's first language to her use of English

81. The ESL teacher has several students with little knowledge of English. How can she best help them develop English competency?

a. Drill verb cases; build vocabulary with a word wall; read the same books repeatedly to build their semantic understanding
b. Incorporate extra-linguistic materials into instruction, such as realia, gestures, and enactments (increased comprehensibility, contextual clues)
c. Have them listen and repeat exercises from a language CD; teach them a "word of the day" and ask them to use it five times in oral or written communication; praise them when they are successful
d. Invite members of a mainstreamed age-appropriate class to visit, and assign each child to a mainstreamed "mentor" to share conversations on topics the ESL children offer

82. "John will identify three physical signs of his anxiety right before introducing himself to a group." This is an example of a behavioral objective for:

a. Emotional exploration
b. Emotional awareness
c. Emotional modification
d. Emotional understanding

83. Young children typically stop demonstrating phonological processes (i.e., typical, normal, predictable, developmental pronunciation errors) at certain ages. Which of the following processes normally ends at the *oldest* age?

a. Saying "big" for "pig" or saying "pick" instead of "pig"
b. Saying "efant" for "elephant" and "tevision" for "television"
c. Saying "one" for "run" and saying "weg" or "yeg" for "leg"
d. Saying "keen" instead of "clean" or "poon" for "spoon"

84. Of the following theories of cognitive development, which proposes discrete developmental changes?

a. Skinner's
b. Vygotsky's
c. Bandura's
d. Piaget's

85. Which of the following is NOT a traditional symptom of laryngeal trauma?

a. Dysphagia
b. Wheezing
c. Hoarseness
d. Hemoptysis

86. Which of the following is true about norm-referenced, standardized test instruments?

a. These tests are better for showing what someone knows than how he or she learns.
b. These tests require much clinical experience and skill to administer and score.
c. These tests retain their validity and reliability regardless of how administered.
d. These tests are equally applicable with linguistically or culturally diverse students.

87. In normal receptive language development, at what age do babies recognize the sound of your voice?

a. 3-6 months
b. 2-4 months
c. 0-3 months
d. Upon birth

88. Which of the following observations does NOT support Chomsky's theory?

a. Children learn a probabilistic model of word sequences through experience.
b. Children in different countries go through similar stages of language development.
c. Children overregularize irregular verbs without having heard any examples of this.
d. Children invent unique languages in the absence of exposure to standard language.

89. Which of the following causes dysphagia for functional rather than obstructive reasons?

a. Diverticulitis
b. Chemoradiation
c. Cervical osteophytes
d. Gastroesophageal Reflux Disease (GERD)

90. Which of the following statements is correct regarding norm-referenced versus criterion-referenced tests?

a. Norm-referenced tests measure more concrete cognitive skills and narrower performance ranges in homogeneous groups, while criterion-referenced tests measure more abstract cognitive skills and wider performance ranges in heterogeneous groups.
b. Norm-referenced tests measure more abstract cognitive levels and wider performance ranges in heterogeneous groups, while criterion-referenced tests measure more concrete cognitive levels and narrower performance ranges in homogeneous groups.
c. Norm-referenced tests measure more concrete cognitive levels and wider performance ranges in heterogeneous groups, while criterion-referenced tests measure more abstract cognitive levels and narrower performance ranges in homogeneous groups.
d. Norm-referenced tests measure more abstract cognitive skills and narrower performance ranges in homogeneous groups, while criterion-referenced tests measure more concrete cognitive skills and wider performance ranges in heterogeneous groups.

91. What is NOT a source of sensorineural hearing loss?

a. Destruction of hair cells in the cochlea
b. Damage to one or more of the ossicles
c. Exposure to excessively loud noises
d. A common progression of old age

92. Which of the following is accurate regarding research findings about SLPs and writing professional reports?

a. Most professors do not expect SLP graduate students to have scientific writing proficiency.
b. Scientific writing instruction is equally effective if given earlier or later in the SLP curriculum.
c. Studies have shown a need for profession-specific writing courses for SLP graduate students.
d. Various studies have found that practice via assignments sufficiently improves writing skills.

93. Which of these tests analyzes both receptive and expressive language?

a. The TACL
b. The ACLC
c. The NSST
d. Peabody

94. A patient who has dysarthria secondary to ALS who can still speak intelligibly, albeit with repetition and effort, is a candidate for a palatal lift prosthetic device under certain conditions. Which of the following accurately represents one of these conditions?

a. Velopharyngeal function and dentition are poor; symptoms progress slowly.
b. Velopharyngeal function is adequate, but the patient manages saliva poorly.
c. Velopharyngeal function is poor, but tongue and lip function are adequate.
d. Velopharyngeal function is adequate, but tongue and lip function are poor.

95. Speech and language disorders and many other problems can be caused by traumatic brain injuries (TBIs). Statistically, which of the following age groups are MOST likely to sustain a TBI?

a. Children aged 5 to 9 years, teens aged 13 to 16 years, and adults aged 75+ years
b. Children aged 0 to 4 years, teens aged 15 to 19 years, and adults aged 65+ years
c. Children aged 7 to 11 years, teens aged 13 to 18 years, and adults aged 50+ years
d. Children aged 0 to 2 years, teens aged 16 to 19 years, and adults aged 80+ years

96. Which is NOT a characteristic of voice differences in the deaf?

a. Overly high pitch before puberty
b. Pharyngeal focus of resonance
c. Severe denasality of the voice
d. True hypernasality with some

97. Which is the most common form of stuttering?

a. Neurogenic stuttering
b. Psychogenic stuttering
c. Developmental stuttering
d. Profound stuttering

98. Which is generally true of diagnostic intervention and dynamic assessment in SLP?

a. It is meant to determine effective treatment without therapeutic benefits.
b. It is meant to build speech-language skills rather than to obtain a diagnosis.
c. It is meant to build speech-language skills and determine effective therapy.
d. It is meant to apply to all children with no benefit to special-needs children.

99. MacWhinney's Competition Model falls into which category of language development theory?

a. Emergentist
b. Empiricist
c. Behavioral
d. Nativist

100. Which of the following statements is true about cultural differences in nonverbal communication?

a. Native American and Middle Eastern cultures require eye contact in conversations.
b. Vietnamese and Hmong cultures value admiration and compliments to their babies.
c. Asian and Hispanic cultures find it rude or disrespectful to make direct eye contact.
d. American and Asian cultures find it affectionate or friendly to pat a child on the head.

101. In Starkweather's (1987) demands/capacity model of stuttering, what is NOT true?

a. Some individuals have a predisposition for their speech to break down.
b. When demands exceed capacity, speech breaks down into dysfluency.
c. Stressors in the social environment do not influence speech demands.
d. Most stutterers report that their speech is "just fine" a lot of the time.

102. Research has found which of the following types of consonants to have the highest rates of correct production in people with cleft palates?

a. Nasal consonants
b. Consonant glides
c. Plosive stops
d. Fricatives

103. Willie is a man in his 50s who sustained brain damage due to head injuries from multiple motor vehicle accidents. He now has motor apraxia. This means that:

a. When he walks, he appears to be drunk.
b. He can use his upper but not lower body.
c. He cannot control external speech organs.
d. He can speak but not understand speech.

104. In an Amish family living in Pennsylvania, a mother tells her daughter, "Sally, eat your mouth empty before you say!" What is this version of the common American English expression "Don't talk with your mouth full" classified as linguistically?

a. A familial variation
b. An idiolectal variation
c. A dialectal variation
d. A regional variation

105. For which of the following students are text-to-speech devices likely LEAST helpful?

a. Students with visual impairments
b. Students with hearing impairments
c. Students with dyslexia
d. ELL students accessing grade-level content

106. How many cranial nerves are there in the human central nervous system?

a. Eight
b. Ten
c. Twelve
d. Fourteen

107. Studies show that, when children start school with language deficits, which of the following is the main cause?

a. These children predominantly come from specific socioeconomic groups
b. These children lack supportive home, peer, and community environments
c. These children predominantly come from particular cultural backgrounds
d. These children mostly represent learners of English as a foreign language

108. A 3-year-old says, "I want 'pasghetti' for supper!" The parent says, "You mean spaghetti?" When the child repeats this correctly, he or she gets spaghetti. Eventually, the child learns to pronounce the word correctly. Regarding learning theories of language development, what is this an example of?

a. Classical conditioning
b. Social learning theory
c. Generative grammar
d. Operant conditioning

109. Which of the following can prevent the MOST common cause for loss of speech due to removal of the larynx?

a. Not screaming a lot
b. Avoiding head injury
c. Lower blood pressure
d. Not smoking tobacco

110. A second-grade teacher is planning a unit on money sense for her English learners. Which of the following best describes a Task-Based Language Teaching (TBLT) approach to promote her students' language development?

a. Students create a chart with the differences between dollars and cents to hang up in class.
b. Students set up shops to sell different creations and use language to buy each other's products.
c. Students bring in actual money from their home countries that they can share with the class.
d. Students complete word problems that will be similar to those used on standardized assessments.

111. An articulation disorder is a ______ disorder affecting the ______ level and involving ______ functions.

a. Speech; phonetic; motor
b. Language; phonemic; cognitive
c. Language; phonetic; motor
d. Speech; phonemic; cognitive

112. How many stages of expressive language development do children go through according to Brown?

a. 4
b. 3
c. 5
d. 2

113. Which statement is true about differentiating velopharyngeal insufficiency versus velopharyngeal incompetence?

a. Velopharyngeal insufficiency is caused by physiological defects; velopharyngeal incompetence is caused by anatomical defects.
b. While differences in symptoms exist, both velopharyngeal insufficiency and velopharyngeal incompetence are caused by anatomical defects.
c. While differences in symptoms exist, both velopharyngeal insufficiency and velopharyngeal incompetence are caused by physiological defects.
d. Velopharyngeal insufficiency is caused by anatomical defects; velopharyngeal incompetence is caused by physiological defects.

114. When determining the "incidence" of a disorder, what is being measured?

a. The number of newly diagnosed cases of the disorder within a given time frame
b. The proportion of the population that currently has the disorder
c. The number of cases of the disorder that were successfully treated
d. The distinct cause of the disorder

115. Which scientific principle explains the decrease in air pressure in response to an increase in airflow as found in the myoelastic aerodynamic theory of phonation?

a. Bernoulli effect
b. Coanda effect
c. Boyle's law
d. Charle's law

116. When a patient who has dysarthria secondary to ALS still can speak intelligibly but often must repeat utterances to be understood, which of the following is NOT a recommended management technique?

a. Having the patient maintain a slow rate of speech
b. Having the patient engage in exercise regularly
c. Having the patient exaggerate all articulations
d. Having the patient use speech amplification

117. Primarily, what is the basic structure of the English language?

a. Isolating or analytic
b. Agglutinating or synthetic
c. Amalgamating or polysynthetic
d. Inflectional or fusional

118. People in the southern United States tend to pronounce the words "pin" and "pen" the same way while people in the northern United States do not because:

a. Southerners were unable to differentiate between their meanings.
b. Nasality often obscures similar vowel sounds.
c. Southern speech has fewer overall vowel sounds.
d. Homophony within a nasal environment can occur in some dialects

119. What is the clinical term for the condition commonly called "tongue-tied"?

a. Glossolalia
b. Microglossia
c. Macroglossia
d. Ankyloglossia

120. What does an 18-month-old child who can follow simple directions but cannot say 25 different words have?

a. An expressive language disorder
b. Normal language development
c. A receptive language disorder
d. A language development delay

121. Which of the following classroom practices is LEAST effective with regard to second language acquisition:

a. Presenting sufficient and meaningful reading and writing experiences for students to practice strategies
b. Keeping all reading and writing activities at the student's current reading level
c. Reviewing and re-teaching as required to ensure that students have integrated essential content
d. Daily introduction of a few new words or concepts

122. Abnormal phonetic patterns in early babbling and later speech are MOST associated with which of these syndromes?

a. Cleft palate
b. Down syndrome
c. Fetal Alcohol Syndrome
d. Sjögren-Larsson syndrome

123. In human anatomical structures related to swallowing, which of the following closes the upper esophageal sphincter (UES)?

a. The pharynx constrictor muscles
b. The submental muscles
c. The pyriform recesses
d. The cricopharyngeus muscle

124. Keith has a behavior disorder and expressive language deficits. His teacher wants to evaluate his progress toward his IEP goals for behavior. Which of the following would be the most appropriate method?

a. Norm-referenced testing
b. Interviewing Keith
c. Observational assessment
d. Curriculum-based testing

125. Which statement is true about strokes and other brain injuries involving the right hemisphere?

a. Such injuries often cause right limb mobility damage.
b. Such injuries often cause cases of visuo-spatial neglect.
c. Such injuries often cause deficits of the right visual field.
d. Such injuries often cause no figurative language problems.

126. Which of the following is NOT one of the ossicles?

a. The stapedius
b. The stapes
c. The malleus
d. The incus

127. The process of hearing differs from the other sensory processes by being entirely ________ rather than ________.

a. Chemical; mechanical
b. Mechanical; chemical
c. Involuntary; voluntary
d. Voluntary; involuntary

128. Jessica is a six-year-old kindergarten student. Which description may indicate typical language development?

a. She speaks in sentences of five to six words.
b. She has a vocabulary of 500 words.
c. She holds up her fingers to tell her age.
d. She uses phrases such as "me want"

129. For treating language disorders via strategy instruction, which of the following represents the right sequence for some of the training steps?

a. Have the individual practice a strategy, then have him or her discuss and rehearse using it.
b. Pretest the individual's strategy knowledge, then describe the strategy, then model its use.
c. Ask the person to try the strategy in different settings, then have him or her practice using it.
d. First model the strategy, then describe it, then have the person practice, then discuss this.

130. Therapy for dysphagia includes all of these EXCEPT?

a. Lip exercises
b. Tongue exercises
c. Mental exercises
d. Swallowing exercises

131. Which of these ideas do the Universalist-Linguistic school of phonological acquisition theories include?

a. Children develop phonological principles in a manner that is not linear.
b. Children develop their phonological concepts through passive learning.
c. Children demonstrate individual differences in phonological acquisition.
d. Children demonstrate their phonological acquisition as active learners.

132. As an SLP conducting an assessment of speech fluency, which of these should you do first?

a. Conduct an oral-peripheral examination
b. Complete a fluency severity rating scale
c. Conduct screenings of hearing and vision
d. Collect family and developmental history

Answer Key and Explanations for Test #1

1. D: ASHA, as well as national and world health organizations, advocate universal newborn hearing screenings because hearing loss is the most prevalent congenital disability and often goes undetected without such screening and because early detection and intervention are crucial to prevent delays in language development and learning resulting from hearing loss. The ages in the other choices are not optimal because they are later than birth.

2. C: The tympanic membrane, or eardrum, is the only part of the hearing mechanism that is actually sensory; that is, it collects sensory information from the sound waves that reach it. The auricle or pinna (A) intercepts sound waves and directs them through the external auditory meatus (B) or ear canal. The ossicles in the middle ear amplify the sound waves and transmit them to the eardrum. The cochlea and Organ of Corti (D) convert the acoustic energy of sound waves into electrical energy, which is transmitted by the auditory nerve to the brain for interpretation.

3. B: Children with Down syndrome have physical characteristics (to greater or lesser degrees) produced by the chromosomal abnormality that causes this genetic syndrome. One such characteristic is a thick, protruding tongue, which can often interfere with perfect articulation of consonants like /s/. Their unclear articulation is not caused by mental characteristics (A): Individuals with Down syndrome can have a wide range of intelligence levels. While there are also some behavioral characteristics associated with Down syndrome (e.g. stubbornness, affection), their articulation is not due to these. As physical stigma associated with Down syndrome and their effects on speech are well established, (D) is incorrect.

4. C: one-on-one stuttering therapy will benefit Erin, but keeping her in the same group is not the least restrictive setting for a student with a high IQ and good grades. Therefore, option A is incorrect.

Grouping Erin with other stutterers is more appropriate than grouping her with students who have delayed language development, but it is still not the least restrictive environment. A small group with other stutterers would be appropriate for pull-out speech therapy sessions but not for the whole school day. Therefore, option B is incorrect.

Because Erin has a high IQ and good grades, Donna is right to advocate for her placement in the general classroom. It is commonplace for students who stutter but have good academic achievement to be in the general classroom. Therefore, option C is correct.

Certainly stutterers have been embarrassed and even humiliated when they stuttered in front of large groups. However, this experience also occurs elsewhere in society, not just in school. Students who stutter are typically not segregated in school to protect them from embarrassment, which would still occur outside the classroom. Donna working individually with Erin would not constitute the least restrictive setting. It would also be impractical in terms of the use of Donna's time. Frequent speech therapy sessions with Donna are indicated, along with having Erin spend the majority of the school day in the general classroom. Therefore, option D is incorrect.

5. A: Manometry is a test wherein a small tube is inserted into the esophagus. The tube is connected at its other end to a computer. While the patient swallows, the tube senses the pressure against it, and the computer program quantifies the amount of pressure. The clinician can then determine whether the esophagus exerts normal pressure during swallowing. Laryngoscopy (B) uses either a fiber-optic laryngoscope or a mirror to view the back of the throat for obstructions or abnormal swallowing function. pH monitoring (C) is a test that measures how frequently stomach acid enters the esophagus and how long the acid remains in the esophagus. This can help diagnose GERD. Esophagoscopy (D), or upper gastrointestinal endoscopy, inserts an endoscope (a flexible, lighted instrument) into the esophagus and sometimes the stomach and small intestine to view and photograph them. The endoscope can also be used to remove tissue for biopsy. This test can detect cancers, polyps, other growths or obstructions, and inflammation.

6. C: Turner syndrome is a chromosomal syndrome wherein a female has a missing or incomplete X chromosome. It can cause hearing and cognitive deficits. Hurler syndrome (A), Hunter syndrome (B), and phenylketonuria (D), which can cause speech or language problems, are all genetic syndromes that are classified as metabolic disorders rather than as chromosomal syndromes.

7. D: Adults who did not lose their hearing until after they had developed speech and language are the best candidates for cochlear implantation. Those born deaf must first learn what sounds are through instruction. Adults who have not obtained enough benefit from using hearing aids are good candidates, whereas those hearing very well using hearing aids (A) are not advised to pursue serious surgery if it is unnecessary. Cochlear implants are considered for adults with severe to profound bilateral hearing loss rather than only moderate loss in one ear (B). Deaf adults who identify strongly with deaf culture (C) frequently refuse to consider any measures to allow them to hear better or hear at all, as they feel being deaf is not a disability and hearing would compromise their deaf identity and belonging to deaf culture.

8. A: In audiology, recruitment means (A) reduced range between an individual's hearing threshold, most comfortable loudness (MCL) and uncomfortable loudness level (UCL). In individuals with normal hearing, the hearing threshold, MCL and UCL are spread far enough apart to tolerate a wide range of loudness levels without discomfort and still hear the stimulus. People with sensorineural hearing loss are more likely to experience recruitment, so there is a much smaller range within which they hear without uncomfortable loudness. Someone who asks a speaker to speak louder and then becomes irritated because the speaker is 'shouting' actually has a very small difference between sounds too soft to here and those so loud they hurt. Recruitment is frustrating for both speaker and hearer as the hearer needs a narrow range of loudness in order to understand what is said without discomfort. The term recruitment does not refer to the phenomenon that at times, nerves or brain tissue can be substituted to serve the same function as the usual tissues when these are damaged (B). It does not refer to the ability of normal hearing acuity to focus well enough to capture barely audible sounds (C). And it does not refer to a wider than normal range between threshold and MCL (D).

9. D: Increasing pauses during turn-taking exercises or conversational speech is an example of a direct therapeutic method for treating stuttering. Changing the stutterer's environment (A) is an example of an indirect therapeutic method. Modifying the speech patterns of the stutterer's parents (B) is an example of changing the stutterer's environment and, hence, is also an indirect treatment method. Focusing on the stutterer's feelings (C), attitudes, and the pragmatics of the stutterer's everyday speech are characteristic of indirect treatment methods.

10. C: One of the impairments that leads to aspiration, most often *during* swallowing, is when the vocal folds do not close adequately, allowing material to pass through them. When liquids enter the pharynx prematurely due to not being contained by the oral cavity (A), this most often causes aspiration *before* swallowing. When the larynx does not close soon enough after a bolus reaches the larynx (B), this also causes aspiration *before* swallowing. When material accumulated in the pharynx is not all swallowed and some remains (D), this can cause aspiration *after* swallowing, when the patient resumes breathing after swallowing and inhales the leftover material.

11. D: Broca's aphasia disrupts the brain's expressive language functions: Patients can understand what others say to them but have difficulty producing their own intelligible spoken language. Difficulty understanding others' questions (A) or statements (B) and discriminating among the speech sounds one hears (C) all indicate problems with receptive rather than expressive language.

12. A: The phonological process of substituting the stop /t/ for the fricative /f/ normally ends around the age of 3 years. The phonological process of substituting the stop /b/ for the fricative /v/ (B) normally stops around the age of 3½ years. The phonological process of substituting the stop /d/ for the affricate /dʒ/ ("j") normally disappears around the age of 4½ years. The phonological process of substituting the stop /t/ for the fricative /θ/ (unvoiced "th") normally is gone by around the age of 5 years.

13. C: Although it may be beneficial to allow her to not be called on in class, this may also cause her to be self-conscious. She might not be comfortable speaking in front of the class, but this strategy may cause her to feel ignored compared to other students. It is important to have a conversation with students like Alison to determine what they are comfortable with and how they can be best supported. Answer A is incorrect because allowing her to use prerecorded audio for presentations might make her feel less stress about talking in front of the class. Answer B is incorrect because giving her the opportunity to collaborate with peers that she knows can help her be supported in the class. Answer D is incorrect because allowing her to sit in front of the class might make it easier to access the teacher.

14. B: The oculomotor (B) nerve, CN III, has the motor functions of visual convergence and accommodation, allowing binocular vision. The trigeminal (A) nerve, CN V, transmits sensations in the eye, nose, and face and also innervates muscles of the tongue and muscles used in chewing. The vagus (C) nerve, CN X, transmits sensations in the ears, pharynx, larynx, and viscera and also innervates muscles of the pharynx, larynx, tongue, and the viscera's smooth muscles. The glossopharyngeal (D) nerve, CN IX, transmits sensations in the tonsils, pharynx, and soft palate and also innervates muscles of the pharynx and stylopharyngeus.

15. D: The expressions quoted are common to urban African-American dialects across the United States. They reflect conventions of this culture. Thus, they are not restricted to a particular region (C). They do not reflect a speech disorder (A), which would be characterized by misarticulation of speech sounds, aberrations in voice quality, or disturbances in rate and rhythm (stuttering). They do not reflect a language disorder (B), which would include problems with word finding or retrieval, constructing complete sentences, processing the spoken language one hears, and so on. (Note: Delayed language development can be attributed to processing disorders, intellectual impairments, and/or environmental deprivation, but it is separate from cultural dialect conventions.)

16. B: Research studies have found that, by counseling their clients as needed, SLPs can also enhance the effectiveness of their therapy that directly addresses speech, language, and hearing impairments. Experts note that the SLP's counseling of clients is not limited to only informing, instructing, and advising (A); it moreover increases treatment efficacy and helps clients to cope with the emotional and psychosocial effects of their speech, language, or hearing impairment. Therefore, (D) is incorrect. It is important for SLPs to remember that the counseling they give their clients does NOT qualify them as psychotherapists, so their counseling does NOT take the place of such services (C). Counseling is within the SLP's scope to help clients cope with the stress of their communication disorders and adapt to the changes they cause but not to resolve all of a client's psychological problems.

17. A: The purpose of an intelligence test is to measure a student's ability to reason and solve problems, which includes thinking abstractly. Intelligence tests can provide valuable information in deciphering the reasons that a student may struggle in particular areas. These tests can be beneficial for students of all grades and disabilities for gathering information. Answer B is incorrect because measuring a student's spoken language abilities would be considered a processing assessment. Answer C is incorrect because measuring a student's ability to convey ideas through oral language would be considered a communication assessment. Answer D is incorrect because visual information assessments would typically fall under the visual-spatial assessment categories.

18. D: Learning theory focuses only on observable behaviors (D). This is why learning theory is also called behavioral theory. B. F. Skinner, a pioneer of learning theory and behavior modification, maintained that what was going on internally in a subject did not matter, not because internal processes and states did not exist, but because they could not be observed or measured and therefore could not be changed in a reliable, measurable way. Unconscious impulses (A) were the focus of Freud's psychoanalytic theory and neo-Freudian theories. Freud believed that the majority of the personality was internalized and hidden, even to oneself. Attempts to understand the unconscious were made through "talk" therapy or analysis of patient interviews, including introspection, free association, slips of the tongue, and dream analysis and interpretation. Internal mechanisms (B), such as Freud's ego defense mechanisms, Chomsky's language acquisition device, and other mechanisms described by other theories, are disregarded in learning theory as they are not outwardly demonstrated or observable. Social relationships (C) are the focus of Erikson's psychosocial theory of development, Vygotsky's theory of sociocultural learning, Bandura's social-cognitive theory and others, but not of learning theory. Behavioral theorists like Skinner would assert that social relationships could be changed in practice by the application of behavior modification principles, but the focus of the theory itself is behavior, not social relationships.

19. B: Problems with syntax (B) involve difficulty forming sentences. Problems with morphology (A) will appear as difficulty forming words. Semantics problems (C) manifest as difficulty understanding words and word relationships. Problems with memory (D) will be evidenced by difficulty with retention, such as remembering spoken messages, and retrieval, such as word finding, fluency, and speech flexibility. Fluency is shown by having words, phrases, and sentences readily available. Flexibility is the ability to shift from one set of words, phrases, and sentences to another set or type, either adaptively in response to external changes or limits, or spontaneously. Other criteria for assessing language ability include creativity and elaboration.

20. A: Variable-ratio (A) reinforcement yields the highest response rate as well as the highest resistance to extinction because reinforcement occurs after an unpredictable number of responses. Variable-interval (B), fixed-ratio (C), and fixed-interval reinforcement (D) all produce a lower resistance to extinction because reinforcement occurs more frequently.

21. C: To encourage the most authentic and comprehensive remediation of language disorders, treatment should be given in as many different settings as possible, including the home, school, and clinical contexts. Early interventions for young children should be in the home rather than a clinic (A). Students should receive treatment not only in school (B), which the law mandates they are entitled to receive at no cost, but also at home, in clinics, and so on. Integrating language goals in classrooms is preferable to pulling students out for separate treatment sessions, and where pull-out programs are used, schools should transition from these to classroom integration of language goals (D).

22. A: This is an example of a behavioral objective written for speech awareness (A). If met, it will demonstrate that John is aware of his dysfluencies 90% of the time. An example of a behavioral objective written for speech description (B) would be: "When asked by the therapist, John will correctly identify the type and place of dysfluency eight out of ten times." This goes beyond awareness to being able to describe the dysfluencies specifically. An example of a behavioral objective written for speech modification (C) would be: "John will implement Speech Target X in three out of four dysfluencies without cueing." (In reality the X would be replaced by the number or letter identifying one of the listed targets developed for that individual client.) This goes beyond awareness and description to independently using a learned technique to modify, or change, one's speech when dysfluency occurs. An example of a behavioral objective written for speech preparation (D) would be: "John will implement Speech Target X without cueing before initiating words he expects to stutter on three out of four times." This goes beyond modifying speech when it becomes dysfluent to preventing the dysfluency by implementing a strategy in advance of stuttering.

23. B: Neurological etiologies for stuttering are supported by research findings that four times as many boys as girls have this speech disorder (A); that twins more often stutter (C); and that more left-handed people stutter than right-handed people (D). These all suggest an association of stuttering with genetic factors. The fact that young children's cognitive development outpaces their motor skills development supports the argument for neurological causes, and the fact that boys' neurological development is slower than girls' is consistent with the fact that far more boys than girls stutter. However, the fact that some children still have persistent stuttering above the age of 6 years (B), when both sexes' motor skills should have caught up with their cognitive development, tends to refute a primarily neurological basis for stuttering.

24. D: Behaviorism (the theory) and behavior modification (the practice) are confined to observable, quantifiable behaviors. This is based on the premise that only an individual's external behaviors, that is, what he or she does, can be observed, measured, and therefore changed by others. Behaviorism and behavior modification do not deny the existence of internal states like thoughts (A), sensory perceptions (B), or emotions (C); they simply exclude these from being recorded or manipulated by others because others cannot observe them. Behaviorism maintains that, what we cannot observe, we cannot reliably measure and thus cannot consistently manipulate or change.

25. A: This person's hearing loss is asymmetrical; that is, it is not of the same degree or configuration in both ears. The left ear has normal hearing at the lowest frequency and moderate loss at the highest frequency, while the right ear has moderately severe loss at the lowest frequency and severe loss at the highest frequency. Hence, the loss is not unilateral (B), that is, in only one ear; both ears have hearing loss at some frequencies. The person does not have symmetrical (C) hearing loss, that is, the same in both ears, because the degree (dB level of loss) and configuration (frequencies where loss exists) are not different in each ear. The loss is not high-frequency (D) because there is also hearing loss at a low frequency.

26. C: Age-appropriate activities for autistic elementary-school-aged children include practice with labeling feelings using stories and cartoons; teaching children to ask social questions of others; having children practice social communication together; modeling nonverbal communication; and using the child's special interests to prolong interactions. Reinforcing the child's response to hearing his or her name called (A) is more age-appropriate for young children with autism. Practicing phrases and strategies for peer interactions (B) is more age-appropriate for preschoolers with autism. Practicing skills for successfully responding in job interviews (D) is more age-appropriate for high school students with autism.

27. B: When the genotype, that is, the genetic composition, for seed color is heterozygous, that is, inheriting two different alleles of the gene, one from each parent, the phenotype, that is, observable physical characteristics, reflects the dominant allele; that is, it masks the existence of the other allele. Recessive alleles can be passed to the next generation, but the trait (seed color in this case) is not apparent when the other allele is dominant.

28. C: Modulation (C) is not one of the four phases of the speech mechanism. Modulation can mean varying the pitch, tone, or intensity of one's voice, which will determine the prosody of a person's speech, but is not one of the actual phases of producing speech. The phases are respiration (A) or breathing, which is required to provide a stream of air; phonation (B) or producing sound by using the air to vibrate the vocal folds and/or other parts of the vocal tract; articulation (D) or altering the specific qualities of phonation to produce various specific vowel and consonant sounds, mainly by changing the shape of the oral cavity as well as manipulating the tongue, teeth, lips to block or release airflow; and resonance, or the natural frequency of vibration of the vocal apparatus.

29. C: The IDEA (Individuals With Disabilities Education Improvement Act) and No Child Left Behind (NCLB) demand greater accountability of educators, including school therapists. Both laws mandate that students with disabilities be included in statewide and district-wide assessments. Before these federal laws increased demands for accountability, students with disabilities were NOT assigned the same curricula as nondisabled students (A). The 1997 and 2004 reauthorizations of the IDEA require disabled students to be included in the general education curriculum. Before these laws were enacted, school performance standards for disabled students were not congruent with standards for nondisabled students. However, with the accountability mandated by the laws, state school systems have had to change this to incorporating grade-level content into their academic performance standards for disabled students, not vice versa (B). Federal law DOES require using any accommodations necessary for the assessment and instruction and treatment of students with disabilities (D).

30. B: According to Principle of Ethics I, Rule J, SLPs can make reasonable statements of prognosis but will NOT directly state or imply a guarantee of results from any treatment or procedure they might provide. This does not mean they should say a prognosis is impossible because the SLP field is too complicated (A); or equate reasonable statements of prognosis with a guarantee (C), which they are not; or confine prognosis statements to standardized test results (D).

31. D: Some dialects in England are characterized by pronouncing words with initial /θ/ (unvoiced "th") as /f/. It is rather common to hear people from England who speak these dialects to substitute /f/ for /θ/. This is NOT an articulation disorder (A), phonological disorder (B), or language disorder (C) to be remediated. It is a normal characteristic of certain regional dialects.

32. C: The period from birth to 3 years is a critical one for children to learn language. Infants and young children must be able to hear others' speech clearly in order to differentiate among various speech sounds. If they cannot, they will have difficulty mastering their own correct production of speech sounds. Even a mild hearing loss can interfere with discrimination of speech sounds, and hence with both clear speech and language development. Therefore, choices (A) and (B) are not true. Research into mild hearing loss demonstrates its correlation with speech and language deficits; hence, (D) is not true.

33. C: Elise's success is most likely due to a combination of Glenda's therapy and Elise's maturation. From third to fourth grade, Elise's vocal apparatus and central nervous system have matured, making her speech more amenable to correction. Additionally, last year's SLP did not try using a physical aid to help interrupt Elise's habitual palatalization (which could have been an incorrect learned behavior, a physiological reflex, or both) and reposition her tongue, nor help her become familiar with how the correct position felt until she could reproduce it. Thus, it is not likely that Elise's correction is due only to maturation or that the treatment did not help (A). She continued to produce the distorted sound until Glenda tried the tongue depressor; thereafter her articulation improved quickly. While Glenda's idea deserves credit, it cannot be said that it was entirely responsible for the results (B) as maturation probably enhanced Elise's ability to respond to the treatment. To say that success was due to a choice Elise made (D) is unfounded; there is much evidence to the contrary.

34. C: Low resistance to the flow of air (C) is not a disadvantage of TEP-inserted prostheses, but an advantage in that it makes vocal production easier than working against higher airflow resistance. Major disadvantages of this treatment include required daily maintenance (A); the need to replace the prosthesis periodically (B); and the expenses associated with this method (D). Another disadvantage is that most patients have to use one hand to block the tracheostoma, similarly to the need to use one hand with an electrolarynx. Other less frequent complications that can occur with TEP prostheses are the formation of granulomatous tissue at the site, which has been reported in about 5% of cases; and aspiration of the prosthesis itself, which is more serious but occurs in only about 1% to 5% of cases.

35. B: According to literature reviews, such as one presented at the 2008 ASHA Convention, research into the topic of teacher referrals to school SLPs is sorely in need of more up-to-date studies. For example, researchers found that some of the studies they reviewed on this topic were conducted in the 1950s, 1960s, and 1970s, not all in the 2000s (D). Not only were these studies respectively over 60, 50, and 40 years old as of 2013; but moreover, speech-language services did not even figure prominently in public school settings during those decades. Another trend observed by those conducting recent literature reviews is that most teachers tend to under-refer students with deficits in areas like voice and articulation rather than over-refer them (A). Moreover, research reviewers find that teachers are often not even cognizant of the clinical implications and concerns of socially withdrawn behaviors and a variety of other student factors rather than being highly aware of them (C).

36. B: Spastic dysarthria means Mary Ellen (B) cannot produce speech sounds. She can vocalize but not verbalize. Her spasticity is a rigidity and incoordination of the muscles used to produce meaningful speech sounds due to damage to the parts of the brain that control these muscles. This term does not mean she is unable to hear speech (A). It does not mean that she cannot understand words (C) or spoken language; this would be a definition of Wernicke's aphasia or receptive aphasia, a neurological disorder that interferes with processing receptive language. It does not mean that she cannot sort or differentiate among speech sounds (D); she can understand what she hears but cannot reproduce it herself.

37. B: Hearing aids amplify sounds; that is, they make them louder; whereas cochlear implants convert sounds from acoustic signals to electric signals—the same thing a normal cochlea does but which a damaged cochlea cannot do. The reverse (A) is incorrect. Neither device transmits {(C), (D)} sound: With hearing aids, the outer, middle, and inner ears still transmit the sound to the brain via the auditory nerve, while hearing aids enable a louder sound to be transmitted. Cochlear implants supplant the hair cells' function of converting sound from acoustical to electrical energy when the hair cells have been destroyed or inactivated, directly stimulating the auditory nerve in their place. Neither device sharpens {(C), (D)} the sound.

38. C: The esophagus (C) is not *normally* most closely involved in speech production. The exception is when a person has had a laryngectomy, i.e. the removal of the larynx, usually in cases of laryngeal cancer. In these cases, the individual cannot phonate normally. Such individuals often learn esophageal speech, wherein they swallow air and then burp, using their other speech production parts to shape this belched air into speech sounds. However, most individuals have intact larynxes and do not use esophageal speech. The body parts most closely involved are the lungs, larynx, trachea, and nasal cavities. The larynx (A) is at the top of the trachea and creates a valve to open and close the air stream. It is used in producing speech and also in coughing, vomiting, urinating, moving the bowels, and heavy lifting. The trachea (B), commonly known as the windpipe, lies vertically between the larynx and the bronchi and in front of the esophagus. It is made up of cartilage rings, fibrous tissue, and smooth muscle, giving it the flexibility to accommodate changes in air pressure within the chest. The nasal cavities (D) are involved in inhaling and exhaling air, producing nasal speech sounds, and contributing to resonance, as well as controlling temperature, humidity, and inhaled particles.

39. B: A fistula that is loose-fitting and capable of expansion (B) is not a desirable characteristic of a good voice prosthesis. When a tracheoesophageal fistula (TEF) is surgically created for the insertion of the prosthesis, it should fit snugly around the inserted device. If the fistula becomes larger with time, this leads to leakage around the prosthesis. According to voice rehabilitation specialists, the characteristics that today's best voice prostheses should have are: (A) safe and reliable use; (C) frontloading insertion, meaning insertion through the tracheostoma rather than the mouth; low resistance to airflow; and (D) semi-permanent fixation, also known as indwelling fixation, whereby the prosthesis has an additional flange to keep it fixed in place so it is not aspirated and does not migrate or move around. This was developed by Panje as a variation of previous prostheses and was refined by Groningen.

40. D: Esophagitis is inflammation of the esophagus. Inflammation can result from the irritation of GERD (gastroesophageal reflux disease), from a pill getting lodged in the esophagus or being difficult to swallow (pill esophagitis), allergic reactions, and so on. The inflammation causes swelling, which narrows or even blocks the esophagus, causing dysphagia. Cleft palate (A), a congenital structural abnormality, causes dysphagia by interfering with lip control in sucking; decreasing oral suction; and importantly, causing velopharyngeal insufficiency resulting in incomplete closure and thus nasal regurgitation. Edentulism (B), that is, the absence of teeth, prevents mastication (chewing); missing some but not all teeth makes chewing less efficient, leaving food boluses larger and harder to swallow. Xerostomia (C), that is, dry mouth or lack of saliva, interferes with the processing of food (saliva contains digestive juices), the formation of food boluses, and bolus transport during eating. Therefore (A), (B), and (C) are not obstructive in nature.

41. C: Amplitude is the maximum change from normal air pressure in the atmosphere created by a sound wave. We perceive relative acoustic amplitude as relative loudness. Period (A) is the time duration a sound wave takes to complete one cycle of vibration. Frequency (B) is how many cycles a sound wave completes per second. We perceive relative acoustic frequency as relative pitch. Wavelength (D) is the distance between the crests or peaks of a sound wave.

42. C: Increased participation by parents and students, as well as increased choices for both, is one area of reform provided by the 2001 No Child Left Behind (NCLB) Act. This law (Title I, Parts A and E) holds not only states but also school districts and individual schools more accountable (A). Another area of reform provided by NCLB is that states and local education agencies are allowed more flexibility in how they use federal education funds rather than being given stricter rules (B). To implement such federal mandates, each state must see that its standards meet or surpass the federal standards to receive federal funds; hence, it is not only federal standards but also state standards (D) that qualify the states for federal funding.

43. D: In none of these practice settings is the SLP alone responsible for making the decision to terminate speech-language therapy. In Birth-to-3 programs (A), the child's third birthday is the criterion for automatic discharge. (The child's discharge planning, in which the SLP may participate, can include transitioning to a preschool program; however, discharge from the Birth-to-3 program is still automatic at age 3.) In public school systems (B), the SLP is required to comply with the IDEA, and only once the multidisciplinary team discusses the impacts of the child's communication status on the child's learning and social skills and makes a collective decision can the child be discharged. In health care systems (C), the paying or accrediting agencies typically affect case management decisions limiting the extent of services; for example, in hospitals. While the SLP may participate in discharge planning, the patient's medical status is the ultimate criterion for discharge determination.

44. D: Neither the parents of the child whose records are accessed nor the employees of the participating agency documenting such records access are included in the IDEA's confidentiality provision regarding record of access (§300.563). The parents and the agency employees are the only exceptions. For all other parties obtaining access to the child's education records, the agency must keep a record of the party's name, the date access was granted, and the purpose for which that party was authorized to use the child's records.

45. C: Individuals with Broca's aphasia (C) have better linguistic comprehension than expression, and it does not remove their ability to employ repetition. Melodic Intonation Therapy (MIT) can be useful for the SLP in this case. MIT is a process where the SLP sings or hums a phrase to the affected individual. The individual then tries to sing, hum, or tap the phrase back to the SLP. MIT would not be an effective treatment for an individual with transcortical sensory aphasia (A) because they have severely impaired auditory comprehension skills, and MIT requires the ability to understand not only what the speaker is saying, but to understand and appreciate their own productions in order to try to repeat them. An individual with Wernicke's aphasia suffers from the same difficulty with comprehension, and would therefore not likely be effectively treated by MIT. Conduction aphasia (D) causes significant impairment of an individual's capacity for repetition, making MIT ineffective.

46. D: Protowords are early "words" used by young children which although they do not exactly match adult words, are still considered early words because the child consistently uses them to represent the same thing. Protowords differ from babbling, which may sound speechlike in its rhythms but does not contain words or protowords. Nonreduplicated babbling (A) means simply that the syllables vocalized are not repeated (e.g., "ba") versus reduplicated babbling, which does repeat syllables (e.g., "ba-ba-ba"). Protowords are features of the early one-word stage, which normally occurs around the ages of 12 to 19 months. The later one-word stage (C) features use of single, more-recognizable adult words like common nouns (e.g., *dog, hat, cup*), proper nouns (e.g., *Mom, Dad, Fido*), common verbs (e.g., *go, sit, come, hug*), and social words (e.g., *please, no, bye-bye*) and typically occurs around the ages of 14 to 24 months (B).

47. B: The least common feature of a functional dysphonia would be (B) an overly loud voice. It is more common in disorders of loudness to find an overly weak, soft, or quiet voice (C). This is thought by some clinicians to reflect shyness, insecurity, and poor interpersonal interactions. Nonetheless, voice therapy to improve respiration and loudness is found more effective than trying to improve the patient's self-esteem and social relationships. Common features of functional dysphonia not related to loudness include breathiness (A), caused by lax approximation of the vocal folds, which may be consistent or only occur with fatigue from overuse; and harshness (D), caused by hard vocal attack, over-approximation of the vocal folds, or by a resonance disorder featuring tongue retraction, pharyngeal constriction, and sometimes nasality.

48. A: ASHA bases its treatment efficacy summaries on data collected from the ASHA National Outcomes Measurement System (NOMS). According to these (2008) data, through SLP treatment, c. 80 percent patients diagnosed with aphasia secondary to left-hemisphere strokes attained one or more levels of progress on the Functional Communication Measures (FCMs—seven-level rating scales from least to most functional, measuring improvement in various clinical areas). The data find that two thirds (i.e., about 67 percent) of preschoolers diagnosed with autism spectrum disorders (B) demonstrated gains of one or more levels on the FCM for Spoken Language Production after SLP intervention. About 70 percent of preschoolers with language disorders (C) were found to gain one or more levels on the FCMs for Spoken Language Production or Spoken Language Comprehension from SLP intervention. Of adults with dysphagia who required feeding tubes (D) when SLP treatment began, about 60 percent no longer needed these and could swallow safely at the end of SLP treatment.

49. A: A case study is an in-depth examination of a specific situation or individual and is a type of descriptive research design. A cohort study (B), a longitudinal study (C), and a cross-sectional study (D) are all examples of correlational research designs. A cohort study (B) examines a population sharing a certain trait over a period time. It is a sub-type of longitudinal study. A longitudinal study (C) observes stability or change in selected characteristics of given individuals over long time periods. A cross-sectional study (D) examines selected characteristics of a given population at one point in time.

50. B: Open-bite (B) in which the upper and lower teeth do not meet is the *most* likely cause of distorted sibilant consonants /s/, /z/, /ʃ/, and /ʒ/. Overbite (A) or supraclusion does not usually cause consonant distortion. Underbite (C) or mandibular protraction, also called mesioclusion, causes no speech distortions when mild. Even when severe, the tongue and lips can usually adjust to accommodate it. A protruding mandible can sometimes cause sibilant distortion, but it is not as frequent. This type of malocclusion can also cause distortion of /f/ and /v/ consonants. Cross-bite (D) can make it harder to produce sibilants by placing the tongue in a poor position for it, but is not as likely to cause distortion except when it co-exists with other problems such as open-bite, motor problems with the tongue, or malformed dental arches.

51. D: The prefrontal cortex is responsible for cognitive functions like attention, planning, reasoning, and judgment, which are necessary to developing language. Neural connections in the prefrontal cortex develop throughout childhood, only attaining maturity following adolescence. Broca's area (A), which is necessary for producing speech, attains maturity in its number of neural connections around the age of 6 to 8 years. This can explain why it is normal if children do not necessarily articulate more difficult phonemes (e.g. /r/, /s/) before this age range, which is, hence, the age norm for these phonemes. Wernicke's area (B), which is necessary for understanding spoken language one hears, normally reaches maturity in its neural connections by the age of 1 year. The hippocampus (C), which is necessary for memory retention, word retrieval, and working memory, which are used in processing language, develops following birth, primarily during the child's second year.

52. D: A medical history (D) may be consulted when developing a lesson plan, but it is not contained within the lesson plan itself. A student will usually have about three goals (A) to work on over the semester. These may be revised during the semester as needed, for example, if the student makes such great progress that they no longer apply or if new information is discovered. Behavioral objectives (B) are ways to achieve the goals. They specifically describe what behaviors the student is expected to perform during a given activity. They can often be changed or adjusted as often as weekly according to the student's performance. The activities the student is to engage in should be described (C) briefly in a lesson plan to give an idea of what you are planning, but not in great detail. You should also list the materials to be used (D) during each separate activity in your lesson plan.

53. B: Typical motor skills development of a 1-year-old includes using the forefinger to point at and/or poke things and people. Cognitive skills (A) of a typically developing 1-year-old include searching for objects he or she has seen that have moved out of his or her sight. Sensory skills (C) of a typical 1-year-old include moving his or her body to music and imitating adult sounds. Language skills (D) of typical 1-year-olds include understanding simple spoken commands and uttering their first words.

54. C: Left-hemisphere brain damage results in aphasia for the majority of right-handed people but for only about half of left-handed people. Therefore, (A) and (B) are both incorrect by reversing these proportions. Because areas in the left and right hemispheres control different areas of language processing, because handedness differentially indicates cerebral dominance, and because lateral innervation is cross-wired with the brain hemispheres, (D) is incorrect.

55. C: People who learn esophageal speech (typically following laryngectomy) well enough are found to have speech that is clearest to the general listener. Buccal speech (A) or "Donald Duck speech," which uses the cheek and jaw to create air pockets, and pharyngeal speech (B), which produces the air supply in the pharynx, are also used by some, but neither is as clear as esophageal speech and consequently not used as often. Because (C) is correct, (D) is incorrect.

56. D: Broca's aphasia affects the expressive language ability to remember and retrieve words, construct sentences with understandable word order and grammar, and otherwise express what one thinks, feels, and needs. Broca's aphasia does not impair receptive (A) language ability, that is, understanding what one hears other people say. This disorder impairs all forms of expressive language rather than differentially affecting certain forms like academic (B) or everyday (C) language.

57. A: Phonology is the branch of linguistics concerning the patterns of speech sounds, their systems, and their rules in any given language. Phonetics (B) is the branch concerning the production, representation, and acoustic properties of speech sounds. Phonemics (C) is the branch concerning the study and development of the specific phonemes (= speech sounds) in any given language. Because only (A) is correct, (D) is not.

58. B: Velopharyngeal mislearning is a cause of phoneme-specific velopharyngeal incompetence: The individual's articulation of certain phonemes is incorrectly pharyngealized or nasalized, causing primarily hypernasal, not hyponasal (C), speech or causing nasal air emission specific to certain phonemes—especially sibilants like /s/. Articulation is often mislearned by individuals with hearing loss (A) due to deficient auditory input, particularly with sibilants, which are harder to hear and see. Velopharyngeal mislearning is always treated by speech therapy but never by surgery (D), as it is not caused by any defect of the speech structures.

59. C: The stapedius reflex protects our hearing from overly loud noises when the stapedius muscle pulls the eardrum and ossicles away from each other to minimize vibration, damping our hearing of the noise. Hence, it does the opposite of amplifying sound (A). This reflex does not activate the stapes (B): The malleus is activated to vibrate by the tympanic membrane (eardrum); the malleus's vibration activates the incus; the incus's vibration activates the stapes. The stapedius reflex, in addition to protecting us from loud noises, damps our hearing of our own voices, which would otherwise block out many other sounds coming from outside of us. Hence, it does not enable us to hear our own voices (D) but reduces this hearing, so we can still hear other sounds while talking.

60. C: In the past, the practice with intellectually disabled clients receiving SLP services was to recommend discharge when the effects of treatment hit a plateau (A) or when the clinician judged that the client had reached a communication level matching his or her level of cognitive development (B). In more recent years, however, experts have come to recommend discharging intellectually disabled clients when they have achieved the ability to transfer the functional communication skills they have learned in therapy to everyday life, as demonstrated by their performing these skills in the context of activities and routines of daily living (C). Both ASHA discharge guidelines and independent clinicians and researchers recommend, in addition to normative standardized test results and functional communication skills, considering the client's opinion (D); however, this applies to clients generally, whereas with the intellectually disabled specifically, some may be able to make and express this judgment with validity, but others may not.

61. B: It is not true that fewer boys are likely to stutter as they age (B). In fact, boys are twice as likely to stutter as girls are (A), and the numbers of boys who continue to stutter as they get older is three to four times as many as girls who continue to stutter as they get older. It is true that the majority of children outgrow stuttering (C), and that only around 1% or fewer of adults stutter (D).

62. A: The normal adult human eating and swallowing processes involve both voluntary and involuntary activities of the muscles and nerves. Therefore, (B), (C), and (D) are all incorrect.

63. B: Semantics is the domain of language involving the meanings of words. To understand and ask "Why" questions involve meaning. Phonology (A) is the domain involving speech sounds and their organization and relationships. Syntax (C) is the domain involving the arrangement of words into phrases, clauses, and sentences. Pragmatics (D) is the domain involving the use of language within social contexts, including its effects on others.

64. A: Part C of the IDEA (Final Regulations, 2011) differentially defines evaluation and assessment. Under Evaluation, all four answer choices are included as required procedures. Answer choices (B), (C), and (D) are related to establishing the student's past speech-language status. Answer choice (A), administering a new evaluation instrument to the student, is related to establishing the student's present speech-language status.

65. C: The accessory (C) nerve, CN XI controls the motor function of the muscles needed to shrug the shoulders and turn the head. The trigeminal (A) nerve, CN V, transmits sensations in the eye, nose, and face and also innervates muscles of the tongue and muscles used in chewing. The facial (B) nerve, CN VII, transmits sensations in the tongue and soft palate and also innervates muscles in the face and the stapedius muscle, which connects to the stapes (stirrup) in the middle ear. The glossopharyngeal (D) nerve, CN IX, transmits sensations in the tonsils, pharynx, and soft palate and also innervates muscles of the pharynx and stylopharyngeus.

66. B: It is most common for children to start losing their deciduous or baby teeth around the age of 7 years. The absence of the two upper middle teeth in front of the tongue interferes with producing /s/; without the dental barrier keeping the tongue in place below the alveolar ridge, the tongue is likely to advance to the interdental position that produces the /θ/ (devocalized "th") and /ð/ (vocalized "th") sounds instead, commonly known as a lisp. Sudden lisping around age 7 is not commonly caused by a developmental disorder (A) or new hearing loss (D) when the child previously had normal articulation. While the age norm for difficult consonants like /s/ (and /r/) is up to 8 years old, and Susan has not yet reached that age, a sudden change from normal articulation to lisping cannot be explained by this; if this were the reason, she would already have been lisping before.

67. D: Of the progressive motor neuron diseases named, only ALS (Lou Gehrig 's disease) causes degeneration in both the upper and lower motor neurons. PBP (A) causes degeneration of only lower motor neurons—specifically the bulbar motor nuclei—not of upper motor neurons. SMA (B) causes deterioration of the spinal anterior horn cells, roots, and nerves—all lower motor neurons, not upper motor neurons. PLS (C) causes deterioration of only upper motor neurons—specifically the motor cells in the cortex and the corticobulbar and corticospinal tracts—not of lower motor neurons.

68. B: The manual for any standardized test should be comprehensive and should include the rationale for the test (A); the qualifications needed for examiners to administer the test (B); a description of how the test was developed (C); and detailed instructions for administering, scoring, and interpreting the test (D), as well as indices of reliability and validity; information about the normative sample; and descriptive statistics, supplemented by visual graphs and informational tables to help examiners understand analysis procedures and more easily interpret the test results.

69. C: Fluency shaping focuses on the stutterer's dysfluent speech and on changing it gradually through behavioral shaping. This includes incremental steps to increase the complexity (C) or length of the client's utterances from one syllable or word to conversational speech. Desensitizing the client from unpleasant emotions about stuttering (A), decreasing the stutterer's anxiety and speech avoidance behaviors (B), and increasing the stutterer's self-confidence and sense of self-worth (D) are all characteristics of the stuttering modification technique.

70. C: Rate (C) is measured when determining speech fluency when diagnosing stuttering, but it is not measured by the ALST. The Adolescent Language Screening Test (ALST; Morgan and Guilford, Pro-Ed, 1984) is designed for ages 11 to 17 years. It takes 10 to 15 minutes to administer. The ALST screens the adolescent's language content, form, and use. It includes seven subscales that respectively measure phonology (D), morphology, sentence formulation, receptive vocabulary, expressive vocabulary (A), concepts, and pragmatics (B).

71. B: Although all of these factors can have a significant impact on a student, the content the student has learned has the greatest impact on the special education identification process. Students may come from many different cultures and have learned different topics and ideas. The special education identification process will look at a student's progress and how much they know about certain subjects compared with their peers. Answer A is incorrect because although the language a student speaks is important, it does not necessarily correspond to whether or not they should receive special education services. Answer C is incorrect because knowing where a student comes from can be helpful, but it does not influence identification. Answer D is incorrect because religion also does not influence identification.

72. A: A *short* palate (A) can lead to inadequate velopharyngeal closure, which results in a hypernasal voice. Surgical trauma (B) can also cause velopharyngeal insufficiency and hence hypernasality, as can accidental injury to the soft palate (C). Some diseases can impair the innervation of the soft palate, and such neurological impairment (D) will also result in velopharyngeal insufficiency and hypernasality.

73. C: Wernicke's aphasia affects the receptive language ability to understand the language one hears others speaking. Wernicke's patients typically can speak fluently (though over time, the meaning of their speech tends to deteriorate due to lack of input and feedback) but cannot understand others' speech. Because patients have more trouble understanding than expressing themselves, Wernicke's aphasia is not an expressive (A) disorder, or a mixed (B), that is, expressive–receptive disorder. This language disorder does not involve an articulation (D) disorder, which affects speech pronunciation rather than language processing.

74. A: In states that license CFs, Medicare requires that the student's supervising SLP cosign the student's clinical reports only in cases when he or she directly supervised the student. Therefore, (C) is incorrect. However, in states that do not license CFs, Medicare considers the clinical fellow a student and requires he or she be supervised 100 percent by a licensed SLP, so the supervising SLP would be required as the qualified provider to sign everything the student writes. Therefore, (B) and (D) are incorrect.

75. B: Semantic classification and categorization (B) would be least applicable to learning synonyms and antonyms. This format is for classifying and categorizing objects, events, or words illustrated in pictures, and for identifying the semantic class to which they belong. Identification, differentiation, and elaboration of meaning (A) is for identifying similarities and differences in word meanings, so it is good for learning antonyms and synonyms. Judgment of consistency of meaning (C) is for identifying words, phrases, or clauses that violate the context (e.g., "The girl washed *itself*. Does this sentence make sense? Can you correct this?" or "The cat was sitting *in* the table. Does this make sense? Can you correct it?"), so it is good for teaching the rules of selection for antonyms and synonyms, as well as pronouns, prepositions, etc. Lexical paraphrasing (D) involves restating sentences by substituting one or more words, so it is also a good format for teaching synonyms (e.g., "Give me another word for...." after presenting a sentence) and antonyms.

76. C: Since Joseph has never walked the route alone, he would get lost if sent out on his own now. Therefore, option A is incorrect.

Sending Joseph out with written directions is not a good idea since he does not have good reading skills. He would likely get lost if he went out alone without prior practice in finding his way. A teacher shadowing him would have to catch up with him to redirect him when he went the wrong way or stopped when he did not know which way to go. Therefore, option B is incorrect.

Since Joseph is used to walking the route with his mother, it would be better to accompany him at first. Doing so would provide a point from which to transition gradually to walking alone. Unlike his mother, the teacher will be prompting him to verbalize the route. Since his expressive language skills are better than his reading skills, this is a more effective modality to help him learn the directions. Therefore, option C is correct.

Gradually decreasing the days his mother goes with him, such as by having her go four days and having him go alone one day, then having her go three days and having him go alone two days, is not a good idea. Joseph's mother has never taught him the route, so he does not know the directions and cannot find his way independently. Since he has always relied on his mother, he would get lost the first time he tried to go on his own. Therefore, option D is incorrect.

77. B: Albert Bandura stated in his Social Learning Theory that people learn by observing others' modeling behaviors and then imitating them. Unlike Skinner's (C) behaviorist theory, which states learning equals a permanent behavioral change, Bandura maintains people may learn new information without exhibiting new behaviors. Bandura finds the conditions or steps required for learning are attention, that is, attending to the modeled behavior; retention, that is, the ability to retain and store observational information; reproduction, that is, practicing and successfully imitating the behavior; and having motivation to imitate the modeled behavior. Piaget (A) maintained that children go through progressive stages of cognitive ability and cannot learn certain concepts until they are developmentally ready to understand them. Vygotsky (D), in his sociocultural theory of learning, emphasized social interactions as the contexts for reciprocal learning and teaching, including the Zone of Proximal Development (wherein a child can do tasks with help that he or she cannot yet do alone) and the concept of scaffolding (a term coined by Jerome Bruner), that is, temporary, gradually withdrawn support.

78. D: The most likely reason for Jason's substitution of glottal stops for many consonants normally shaped in the mouth with the aid of the tongue and teeth is that (D) the newborn's jaundice and lethargy were most likely symptoms of a virus which caused minimal neurological damage. This kind of damage can slightly impair specialized functions such as motor functions related to the oral apparatus. He may have sustained subtle damage to the glossopharyngeal nerve (CN IX), the vagus nerve (CN X), the accessory nerve (CN XI), and/or the hypoglossal nerve (CN XII) involved with the muscles of the pharynx, larynx, tongue, and soft palate. It is not likely that he is merely being lazy (A) as it is developmentally normal for a child to use the apparatus best suited to imitate the sounds he hears. The fact that Jason substitutes glottal stops for *many* consonants means it is not likely that this speech dysfunction will correct itself without treatment (B). Glottal stops are not features of many consonants in English, making Jason's substitution for many consonant sounds unusual. It is not likely that Jason simply formed a habit he did not grow out of (C) as making this substitution is not natural. He would be more likely to employ the usual oral structures. The glottal stops take more effort even though he is fluent.

79. B: AAIDD is the American Association on Intellectual and Developmental Disabilities. Typically a speech-language pathologist and audiologist will work with students who do not have intellectual disabilities as well as with those who do. She might have an AAIDD membership as well, but this would not be the primary choice of those listed. Therefore option A is incorrect.

ASHA is the American Speech and Hearing Association. This is the most logical primary choice for Ms. Banus. Therefore option B is correct.

APA is the American Psychological Association. Ms. Banus is not a psychologist or behavior specialist. Thus she is unlikely to be a member of this organization. Therefore option C is incorrect.

CCBD is the Council for Children with Behavioral Disorders. Ms. Banus has an equal probability of working with some students who also have behavior disorders and with many other students who do not. She does not specialize in behavioral disorders. Therefore option D is incorrect.

80. D: Students learning English as a foreign language frequently transfer incompatible properties and rules of their native languages to English. This is one example. The Chinese language does not add plural endings the way the English language does, so native Chinese speakers often leave off the –*s* in plural English words. While being unfamiliar with English (A) contributes to this error, the error is not *most* due to it: Lack of familiarity alone would produce more random types of errors, while transfer from the native language confers the specific error type described. The error is not due to a language disorder (B), which would produce a variety of errors rather than this specific one. Tina's error is not idiolectal (C) as it is not individual to her; it is a very common error among Chinese-speaking people when they learn English.

81. B: Incorporate extra-linguistic materials into instruction, such as realia, gestures, and enactments. Comprehensibility will be increased by direct, hands-on involvement and clues to meaning that exist in the physical context of the classroom.

82. B: This is an example of a behavioral objective written for a stutterer in the area of (B) emotional awareness. If met, it will show that John is aware of his anxiety and the associated symptoms in this type of situation. An example of a behavioral objective for emotional exploration

(A) is: "When asked by the therapist, John will describe in detail three childhood experiences that triggered negative emotions." Once he is aware of his emotions related to stuttering, John can explore them to see how they may have developed and been compounded over time. An example of emotional modification (C) is: "On three separate occasions, before speaking to a group, John will pause, take a deep breath, slowly exhale, and attend to the release of muscle tension in one part of his body." This is a part of progressive relaxation practice. Once John recognizes his emotional reactions, he can practice changing them by focusing on the physical tension they cause and releasing it. The effects are reciprocal; just as anxiety causes muscular tension, releasing that tension reduces the anxiety. An example of a behavioral objective written for the area of emotional understanding (D) is: "With the therapist's assistance, John will form one plausible reason for his stuttering and will express it to someone outside of therapy." This reflects gaining insight into reasons for stuttering.

83. C: This is an example of changing liquid phonemes like /r/ and /l/ into glides like /w/ and /y/. The age norm for this phonological process to end in normally developing children is around 5 years. Voicing unvoiced initial consonants like "big" for "pig," or devocalizing voiced final consonants like "pick" for "pig" (A) are phonological processes that both normally end around the age of 3 years. The phonological process of deleting weakly stressed syllables like the "le" in "elephant" or "television" (B) normally ends around the age of 4 years. The phonological process of reducing consonant clusters by omitting one consonant (D) also normally stops around the age of 4 years.

84. D: Piaget's theory posits four distinct stages of cognitive development, each with specific distinguishing characteristics and corresponding to approximate age ranges. Skinner's (A) theory of cognitive development is behavioral. It does not include stages but focuses on the premise that changes in behaviors over time represent learning and that this learning occurs through the antecedent and consequent events immediately before and after a behavior, which increase or decrease the probability of the individual's repeating the behavior. Vygotsky's (B) theory also has no stages and focuses on sociocultural influences as sources of learning. Bandura's (C) social learning theory has no stages either; it focuses on learning through observation, imitation of models, and vicarious learning.

85. B: Wheezing is not a common symptom of laryngeal trauma. Common signs of laryngeal trauma include dysphagia (A), hoarseness (C), and hemoptysis (D). Wheezing (B) tends to indicate an issue with the lungs rather than the structures of the neck.

86. A: Most norm-referenced, standardized tests tend to be static by measuring what someone knows rather than dynamic by showing how one learns. This can be a disadvantage. However, an advantage of these tests is that they do NOT require extensive clinical experience and skill to administer and score (B). They include manuals with clear instructions for administration, scoring, and interpretation. While standardized, norm-referenced tests have been vetted for validity and reliability before publication, if they are not administered exactly according to the instructions, this can compromise the validity and reliability of the results. Another caveat with standardized tests comparing scores to representative sample populations is that they may be inappropriate to give to linguistically and culturally diverse students (D), whose knowledge and experience differ from those of the sample populations.

87. C: Babies will respond to the sound of any voice upon birth (D) and show recognition of a familiar voice between birth and 3 months of age by smiling or stopping their crying when they hear it. Normally developing babies will do this before they are 4 (B) or 6 (A) months old.

88. A: The observation that (A) children learn a probabilistic model of word sequences through experience supports statistical learning theories of language development, not Chomsky's theory. In statistical learning theory, children develop an understanding of the probability of how words will likely appear in a sequence through experience and generalize their learning to patterns and categories of word order. The observation that children with different languages go through similar developmental stages in learning language (B) supports Chomsky's theory of universal grammar. Overregularization of irregular verbs, such as "goed" or "taked," reflects a basic understanding of how regular verbs conjugate. Children applying the rule to irregular verbs without having heard such constructions supports Chomsky's theory of inherent linguistic structures. The observation that children may invent unique languages when not exposed to a standard language (D) supports Chomsky's theory of innate devices enabling language development. Researchers found a group of deaf children in Nicaragua who could not hear spoken Spanish and were never taught any standard sign language. These children invented their own sign language, which was grammatically complex and was not related to Spanish or to any standard sign language.

89. B: Chemoradiation therapy to treat cancer of the head and neck can frequently cause delays in the initiation of swallowing, decreases in pharyngeal transport of food, and inadequate protection of the larynx. These are all functional impairments in swallowing. Diverticulitis (A) consists of diverticula, or pouches, forming in the walls of the digestive tract, including the esophagus or pharynx. This cause is obstructive. Cervical osteophytes (C) are bone spurs that grow out from the cervical vertebrae and are more common in elderly patients. These can restrict the food pathway and move food toward the airway. This is also an obstructive cause. GERD (D) involves stomach acid repeatedly backing up into the esophagus, which can create esophageal ulcers. These ulcers can cause scar tissue formation, narrowing the esophagus. This is also an obstructive cause of dysphagia.

90. B: Norm-referenced tests are better for measuring more abstract, higher cognitive levels; for testing heterogeneous (mixed) groups; and for testing a wide range of performance in groups with broad ranges of skills. Conversely, criterion-referenced tests are better for measuring more-concrete, lower cognitive levels; for testing homogeneous (uniform) groups; and for testing a more limited range of performance in groups with narrower ranges of abilities.

91. B: Damage to one or more ossicles (B) is not a source of sensorineural hearing loss but a source of conductive hearing loss. Damage to any of the middle ear's tiny bones, stopping them from vibrating and sending sound through the oval and round windows to the inner ear, will impede conduction of sound and cause conductive hearing loss. Destruction of hair cells in the cochlea (A) is a source of sensorineural hearing loss. It can also be caused by sudden or ongoing exposure to excessively loud noises (C), by disease or infection, or as a result of aging (D).

92. C: Research finds that graduate students in SLP preparation programs are not automatically proficient in the scientific writing skills they will need for writing professional reports, indicating a need for more profession-specific writing courses in SLP graduate curricula. Research finds that most professors actually DO expect these graduate students to be proficient in such writing skills without having been taught them (A). Research finds that, when SLP graduate students do receive such instruction, it occurs later in their curricula; yet, studies also show that such instruction received earlier in the curriculum benefits SLP students more by giving them more practice and skills refinement, so it is NOT equally effective whether given earlier or later (B). Research furthermore finds that practice via writing assignments alone does NOT improve students' scientific writing skills (D).

93. C: The NSST (C) or Northwestern Syntax Screening Test has two sections, Receptive and Expressive. The TACL (A), or Test for Auditory Comprehension of Language, contains sections on Vocabulary, Morphology, and Syntax, but only tests the receptive side of language. Its format requires a child to point to one of several pictures that best illustrates the meaning of the word, phrase, or sentence spoken by the tester. The ACLC (B), or Assessment of Children's Language Comprehension, also assesses basic receptive language skills. It includes a section of vocabulary words and three sections of syntactic sequences (phrases or sentences). It also requires the child to point to the correct choice among several. The Peabody (D) Picture Vocabulary asks the child to point to one of several pictures to identify which word (or occasional short phrase) the examiner has spoken as well.

94. C: The palatal lift is a prosthetic device that helps to lift up the palate in patients with poor velopharyngeal function. It is hence not indicated for those with adequate VP function {(B), (D)}. Patients' symptoms should be progressing relatively slowly (A) for them to be palatal lift candidates; however, this device is not indicated for patients with poor dentition (A) because their teeth must be adequate to support the prosthesis. The patient should also still be able to manage his or her salivary secretions adequately (B) to use this device. While the palatal lift is indicated to manage decreased VP function, the patient should still have adequate use of the tongue and lips rather than poor tongue and lip function (D).

95. B: According to the Centers for Disease Control and Prevention (CDC, 2010, 2012), children from the ages of birth to 4 years, adolescents from the ages of 15 to 19 years, and adults aged 65 years and older are the age groups found most likely to incur traumatic brain injuries (TBIs).

96. A: Deaf children around the ages of seven or eight years old have not been observed to speak with higher pitches than hearing children. However, children with hearing develop lower-pitched voices after puberty, while deaf children do not (A). Researchers have concluded this is because they do not have the auditory feedback that hearing children do and thus cannot acoustically monitor their voices. It has been found that deaf individuals without voice training tend to focus their resonance in their pharynx (B), caused by poor tongue positioning, especially retraction toward the pharyngeal wall, leading to "cul de sac resonance." Severe denasality (C) often results from pharyngeal resonance focus, but there are also some deaf people who display true hypernasality (D) in their voices.

97. C: The most common form of stuttering is (C) developmental stuttering. When young children are still developing speech and language skills, they may stutter. Some scientists believe that this is due to a child's cognitive and verbal development outpacing that child's speech and language development. Neurogenic stuttering (A) is not as common as developmental stuttering but more common than psychogenic stuttering (B). Neurogenic stuttering is a result of a neurological problem. This can be caused by head trauma, cerebrovascular stroke, or other brain injuries. The stuttering arises from an impaired ability of the brain to coordinate speech actions by properly controlling the muscles and/or nerves involved. Psychogenic stuttering (B) is a result of emotional trauma, emotional problems, mental disorders, and/or cognitive impairments. In the past, stuttering was believed to be always psychogenic in origin. However, now that more research has been done, it has been found that psychogenic stuttering is actually not common. Profound stuttering (D) is a label of severity rather than a category of form and is therefore incorrect.

98. C: Diagnostic interventions, also sometimes called *dynamic assessments,* generally serve the dual purpose of building a child's speech-language skills while testing for which interventions are effective for that child via a Response-to-Intervention (RTI) model. So-called dynamic assessments offered by some clinicians also can benefit special-needs children (D) who cannot successfully perform on standardized test instruments. The dynamic assessment has the advantages of specialization and individualized observations not possible with standardized tests.

99. A: MacWhinney's Competition Model is an (A) emergentist theory of language development. Such theories claim that language acquisition is a cognitive process emerging from the interactions of biology and the environment. Empiricist (B) theories arose as a reaction against nativist theories which emphasized the innate nature of language acquisition. These include relational frame theory, social interactionist theory, statistical learning theories, and functional linguistics. Empiricism recognizes the interaction between nature and nurture, but puts more emphasis on the role of learning, or nurture, and finds that the inherent, or nature, part is a general cognitive learning mechanism. Behavioral (C) theories such as Skinner's find language acquisition to be a form of operant conditioning in which linguistic behavior is shaped by the consequences of verbal responses. Nativist (D) theories include Chomsky's transformational grammar or generative grammar and the theories of Jerry Fodor and Eric Lenneberg. These theories view the acquisition of language as being based more on inherent abilities or mechanisms than on environmental influences.

100. C: In Asian and Hispanic cultures, as well as Middle Eastern and Native American cultures, people find it rude or disrespectful to make direct eye contact when talking with others. Therefore, (A) is not true. This attitude contrasts with Western mainstream cultures, which teach us that, when talking to people we should "look them in the eye." Contrary to the value Western cultures place on people's admiring and complimenting their babies as beautiful or cute, Vietnamese and Hmong cultures avoid such behavior (B) because they fear that a spirit overhearing the compliments will try to steal or harm the baby. And, while American cultures view patting children on the head as affectionate or friendly, Asian cultures do not (D): They believe the head is a sacred body part that should not be touched by others.

101. C: It is not true in Starkweather's model that (C) stressors in the social environment do not influence speech demands. Social stressors are an important factor according to Starkweather. Speech is a social behavior. Starkweather states that stressors, or demands, in the social environment can trigger stuttering when those demands exceed the capacity of the individual to speak fluently and continuously (B). These demands trigger the stuttering rather than causing it; Starkweather believes that some people have a predisposition for speech breakdowns (A). These predispositions are thought to be genetic in some people, while in others they may not be hereditary but are results of weaknesses in the speech process involving muscular control, motor coordination, word finding, sentence formation, or auditory monitoring. It is true that most stutterers report that their speech is "just fine" a lot of the time (D), but they will stutter in stressful situations such as talking to a superior, talking on the phone, making a presentation, or in a job interview.

102. A: Research has found that people with cleft palates consistently have the highest rates of correct production of (A) nasal consonants like /m/, /n/, and /ŋ/. This makes sense when one considers that one of the byproducts of cleft palate is hypernasality. It would follow that it is easier for people whose speech is already nasal to produce nasal consonants correctly. The second highest ranking of correct articulation for those with cleft palate was (B) glides or semivowels like /r/, /l/, /j/, or /w/; the third was (C) plosives or stops like /p/, /b/, /t/, /k/; ranked fourth highest were (D) fricatives like /θ/, /ð/, /s/, /z/, /f/, /v/.

103. C: The best definition of motor apraxia among the choices given is that (C) he cannot control his external speech organs. For example, when asked to make an /m/ sound, someone with motor apraxia is unable to. When the SLP models using thumb and forefinger to pinch the lips together,

Willie will be able to imitate, but he cannot voluntarily press his lips together without the aid of his hand. If he walked as if he were drunk (A), it is a sign of *ataxia* rather than apraxia. If he used his upper but not lower body (B), it is hemiplegia. If he can speak but not understand speech (D), it indicates Wernicke's aphasia or receptive aphasia. None of these other conditions exist in this case. Apraxia means loss of ability to make simple voluntary acts, *especially* loss of ability to perform simple units of action in expressive language.

104. C: This expression reflects the dialect of the Amish people, a subcategory of Mennonites descended from Swiss and Alsatian Anabaptists who followed Jakob Ammann (hence the name Amish). The English spoken by the Amish is influenced by their German-speaking ancestry and preserved by their insular communities. The expression is not familial (A) because it is not specific to one family but common to the Amish as a group. It is not idiolectal (B), that is, specific to one individual's speech. It is not regional (D) because the Amish do not live exclusively in a region of Pennsylvania or even the whole state; there are also substantial Amish populations residing in Ohio, Indiana, New York State, and Canada, especially Ontario.

105. B: Text-to-speech software is often helpful for those who have reading disabilities, such as dyslexia, those with visual impairments, and those who have trouble reading due to a lack of English mastery. Students with hearing impairments likely would not benefit from such devices, as they may have trouble hearing them.

106. C: There are twelve (C) cranial nerves in the human CNS. They are: I – olfactory; II – optic; III – oculomotor; IV – trochlear; V – trigeminal; VI – abducent; VII – facial; VIII – auditory or acoustic; IX – glossopharyngeal; X – vagus; XI – accessory; and XII – hypoglossal. There are not eight (A), ten (B), or fourteen (D) cranial nerves, so these answers are all incorrect. A helpful mnemonic that many medical students use to remember these nerves is: "On Old Olympus' Towering Top, A Finn And German Viewed A Hop." The initial letters of each word correspond to the initial letters of each nerve.)

107. B: Research finds that the main cause of children starting school with language deficits is because their home and community settings and peer groups do not provide sufficient support or opportunities for language development. Language deficits are NOT found to prevail among certain socioeconomic groups (A), cultural backgrounds (C), or ESL/ELL children (D). Researchers point out that children from wealthy families can be deficient in language skills as well as those from poor families and that ESL/ELL children can excel in English at school just as native English-speaking children can perform below average scholastically. The prevalence of language deficits in ESL/ELL settings is more due to many of these children's English exposure being limited to school lessons.

108. D: Operant conditioning is included in learning theories of language development, which are based in behaviorism. When the parents give the child spaghetti after he or she repeats the correct pronunciation, they are selectively reinforcing (rewarding) the desired behavior. Classical conditioning (A) is also a learning theory but involves conditioning via association. For example, if the parents say "spaghetti" every time they serve it, eventually, the child responds the same way to hearing the word alone as to the food. Another learning theory is social learning theory (B), which states children need not receive reinforcements directly but learn from observing and then imitating models like their parents (and observing others being rewarded for certain behaviors and then imitating these). Generative grammar (C) is NOT a learning theory: It is a feature of nativist theories like that of Noam Chomsky, which propose children have innate abilities, like a Language Acquisition Device (LAD) and a Universal Grammar, for developing language rather than learning language via interactions with the environment, as learning theories propose.

109. D: Smoking tobacco (in cigarettes, cigars, and pipes), as well as chewing or "dipping" (holding between cheek and gum) tobacco, is a primary cause of laryngeal cancer (as well as cancers of the lips, mouth, tongue, salivary glands, esophagus, stomach, etc.). A common treatment for laryngeal cancer is laryngectomy. With removal of the larynx, the voice is lost. Avoiding screaming (A) can prevent most vocal cord nodules and some vocal cord polyps, which cause voice problems but not laryngectomy. Avoiding head injuries (B) can prevent vocal cord paralysis, which can occur secondary to head and neck trauma as well as to various diseases, tumors, certain surgeries, and strokes. Strokes are often secondary to high blood pressure, so lowering it (C) can prevent strokes, which can cause not only vocal cord paralysis but also aphasias, apraxias, and dysarthrias, which all affect speech and language. However, strokes do not lead to laryngectomies.

110. B: The Task-Based Language Teaching (TBLT) approach uses real-life examples and tasks to teach language. When teaching about money, the TBLT approach should consider how money is used in the real world and emulate scenarios in which students will use money, such as buying and selling products. Several of these activities can be helpful in developing money sense; however, they do not use the TBLT approach. Bringing in actual money may be inclusive of different cultures and focus on realia, but beyond actual objects, TBLT focuses on scenarios and situations.

111. A: Articulation disorders are *speech* disorders, affecting the *phonetic* level, which involves the *motor* functions needed for correctly producing vowel and consonant speech sounds. Language disorders that affect the *phonemic* level, which involves the *cognitive* functions needed for correctly organizing one's speech sounds into a system of phonemic or sound contrasts, are phonological disorders. (Note: Many people, including even SLPs, use these terms incorrectly or interchangeably.)

112. C: According to Brown (1973), children go through five stages in expressive language development: Stage I typically takes place between 12 and 26 months. Stage II typically occurs between 27 and 30 months. Stage III typically occurs between 31 and 34 months. Stage IV typically occurs between 35 and 40 months. Finally, Stage V occurs between 41 and 46 months.

113. D: Both velopharyngeal insufficiency and velopharyngeal incompetence cause inadequate functioning of the velopharyngeal closure, that is, of velopharyngeal dysfunction in general. However, velopharyngeal insufficiency is caused by anatomical defects, such as an overly short palate; a lack of tissue (as during repair of cleft palate); a submucous cleft; cranial base anomalies causing a deep pharynx; sequelae of adenoidectomy, and so on. But, velopharyngeal incompetence is caused by physiological deficits, such as hypotonia of the pharynx; paresis or paralysis of the velum; poor overall muscle tone; or neurological conditions affecting speech movements, for example, dysarthria or apraxia, and so on.

114. A: Incidence (A) is the measure of newly diagnosed cases of a particular disorder within a specified time frame. Prevalence is the proportion of the population that currently has the specified disorder (B). A measure of successful treatments (C) is typically known as a success rate or cure rate. The distinct cause of a disorder (D) is the etiology.

115. A: According to the myoelastic-aerodynamic theory of phonation, the adducted vocal folds create resistance against the exhaled air. Air pressure below the glottis then builds up, opening the vocal folds. The subglottic pressure is then immediately released as airflow. This increased air velocity causes air pressure to drop relative to the vocal folds' medial (inner) borders, which brings the vocal folds back together again. This air pressure decrease corresponding to the increased air speed that causes the vocal folds' approximation is known as the Bernoulli effect (A). All of the other principles are unrelated.

116. B: According to the research, there is no evidence that exercising helps dysarthria symptoms in ALS patients, and there is even some evidence that it can harm them. Therefore, such patients who can still speak should be advised to conserve their remaining energy. These patients should also be encouraged to speak at a slow rate (A) consistently, to exaggerate their articulation (C) of speech sounds and articulate them as precisely as possible, and to consider introducing the use of amplifiers (D) to make their speech louder so others can hear and understand them better.

117. D: English has primarily* an inflectional/fusional language structure; that is, it adds regular prefixes and suffixes to words to vary their meaning but also varies words for this purpose. Due to its many irregular forms, English and some other inflected languages are hard to learn. Languages with isolating/analytic (A) structures include Chinese, Indonesian, and Creole and Pidgin languages. These feature invariable words and strict syntactical rules. (*Note: While English is primarily inflectional, it has begun to evolve some analytic/isolating features.) Adults find analytic languages easier to learn than children do. Agglutinating/synthetic (B) languages include Turkish, Japanese, Finnish, Tamil and others. They are easy for children to learn. Their prefixes and suffixes are very regular. Amalgamating/polysynthetic (C) languages include Basque and many Native American tribal languages. They feature complex words, each imparting as much information as a sentence and are very hard to learn.

118. D: The "pin"/"pen" phenomenon is an example of (D) homophony in a nasal environment which occurs in some dialects, such as Southern American English. The nasality of the /n/ following the vowel in both words causes the vowels to sound the same in this regional dialect. The idea that the nasal /n/ sound obscures the distinction between /I/ and /ɛ/ (B) sounds plausible but is untrue. Southern speech does not have fewer vowel sounds (C) than Northern speech; many vowels are pronounced as diphthongs or triphthongs in the South, suggesting more vowel sounds. It is wholly untrue that Southerners do not know the meanings of these words (A), as evidenced by a common response in Southerners when hearing either word without sufficient context to distinguish the meaning; i.e. "Do you have a pen/pin?" will often be met with the response, "Do you mean an ink pen or a safety pin?" Linguists have demonstrated the homophony phenomenon with native Southerners by asking them to make a conscious effort to pronounce each vowel differently in isolation while nasalizing their speech; most cannot, producing the same vowel sound each time.

119. D: *Ankyloglossia* (from the Greek for "crooked tongue") is the clinical term for "tongue-tied." It is usually caused by an abnormally short frenulum, the piece of tissue connecting the tongue to the bottom of the oral cavity. Depending on its severity, it can cause articulation problems. *Glossolalia* (A) (from the Greek for "tongue babble") is the clinical term for speech composed of unintelligible syllables that sound like speech but are meaningless. It can be a symptom of schizophrenia. It also describes the "speaking in tongues" of some religious groups. *Microglossia* (B) (from the Greek for "small tongue") is an abnormally small tongue, a congenital deformity. *Macroglossia* (C) (from the Greek for "large tongue") is an abnormally large tongue, characteristic of Down syndrome and Beckwith-Wiedemann syndrome, and can also be secondary to hypothyroidism, amyloidosis, and acromegaly.

120. B: Receptive language develops sooner than expressive language. Children must understand the language they hear before they can produce their own. A normally developing 18-month-old is hence able to follow simple directions but will only utter a few words. Being able to use 25 words or more is typical of a normally developing 2-year-old. The child described therefore does not have an expressive (A) or receptive (C) language disorder. Neither does this child have delayed language development (D).

121. B: Presenting sufficient and meaningful reading and writing experiences for students to practice strategies and reviewing and re-teaching as required to ensure that students have integrated essential content are part of scientifically-based, quality classroom instruction. Daily introduction to new concepts, words, and materials can be okay as long as they are integrated a little at a time. Students require multiple exposures to a word before recognition begins to happen automatically. This relies on Krashen's input hypothesis, which states that learners benefit from exposure to slightly more difficult language than their current level. This renders answer choice B as the least effective, since it implies only using a level of language that the student is comfortable with.

122. A: In children with cleft palates, research has found phonological deviations in their early babbling patterns, and phonetic deviations can continue in their speech as they grow older. Down syndrome (B) commonly causes an overly large, thick tongue, causing articulation difficulties and often causes delayed language development secondary to intellectual disability. Some Down syndrome children are found to show phonetic deviations as well as delays, but the former are not as notable as with cleft palate. Fetal Alcohol Syndrome (C) is associated with poor articulation, slurred speech, fluency deficits, absence of intonation, and voice dysfunctions, but not particularly with phonetic deviations. Children with Sjögren-Larsson syndrome (D) tend to have dysarthria and delayed speech-language development secondary to intellectual disability. They are more likely to be able to speak very little or not at all than to demonstrate abnormal phonetic patterns.

123. D: The cricopharyngeus muscle is attached from the front to the sides of the cricoid cartilage. This muscle compresses the UES against the rear of the cricoid cartilage, causing it to close. The pharynx constrictor muscles (A) are a layer of muscles on the pharynx that begin on the cranium, the hyoid bone, and the front of the thyroid cartilage. They insert onto a posterior median raphe. The submental muscles (B) begin on the mandible (lower jaw) and attach to the hyoid bone and the tongue. The pyriform recesses (C) are not muscles; they are two spaces found in the pharynx, positioned laterally to the larynx.

124. C: Any kind of observational assessment will involve direct observation of Keith's behavior, which is what the teacher wants to evaluate. If the teacher uses the same recording methods as for behavioral baseline measures, comparing current results to baseline can indicate Keith's progress. Norm-referenced tests (A) are standardized tests and typically measure academic achievement, not behavior. Interviewing Keith (B) is contraindicated because he has expressive language deficits and may have difficulty responding, and also because observing what the student does is more accurate than asking the student to describe his own behavior. Curriculum-based testing (D) connects assessment to instruction. While behavioral interventions have probably been incorporated during Keith's classroom instruction, curriculum-based assessments are related to curriculum content areas, not behavioral issues.

125. B: Right-hemisphere neurological damage from strokes and other traumatic brain injuries can often cause symptoms of visuo-spatial neglect, cause damage to the mobility of the LEFT limbs (A), cause LEFT visual field deficits (C), and DO often cause impairment in the ability to understand figurative language (D)—that is, expressions like irony, sarcasm, jokes, puns, other wordplay; metaphors, similes, alternate meanings; and other nonliteral figures of speech and subtle nuances of language. Damage to one hemisphere typically (with some exceptions) causes problems on the opposite side of the body due to the cross-wiring of body part innervations with the opposing cranial nerves.

126. A: The stapedius (A) is not one of the ossicles, though it is attached to one. "Ossicles" means "little bones." These tiny bones in the middle ear perform the function of conducting sound from the external auditory meatus to the inner ear. They are the stapes (B) or stirrup, the malleus (C) or hammer, and the incus (D) or anvil. When sound enters the ear, the malleus strikes the incus, vibrating the stapes. The stapedius (A) is a muscle that attaches to the stapes. In the event of a sudden, very loud sound, the stapedius muscle pulls the stapes away from the incus, keeping the middle and inner ear from registering the full loudness and protecting against sustaining noise-induced hearing loss. This action by the stapedius muscle is called the stapedius reflex.

127. B: The process of hearing is entirely mechanical, while the processes of seeing, smelling, tasting, and touching all include chemical reactions rather than vice versa (B). Both voluntary and involuntary actions are involved in the complete hearing process (including the brain's auditory processing) rather than just one or the other {(C), (D)}.

128. A: By the age of six, typical language development will include speaking in sentences of about five or six words. By this age, children tend to have a vocabulary of 2,000 or more words, so answer choice B is incorrect. Children at age six are also expected to communicate their age orally rather than with their fingers, so answer choice C is incorrect. They also no longer say simple phrases such as "me want," which eliminates answer choice D.

129. B: The SLP should first pretest the individual for prior knowledge about any strategy to aid in performing various language tasks. Then, the SLP should give the individual a description of the strategy, then model it for the learner, then have the learner discuss and rehearse the strategy, then have the learner practice using it, and then assign the learner to apply the strategy to different settings until the skill becomes generalized across situations.

130. C: Mental exercises (C) are not part of the traditional set of dysphagia therapies. Lip exercises (A) increase strength and coordination of the lips, which are important for moving food around the mouth and for creating a tight seal when swallowing. Tongue exercises (B) are helpful because the tongue also moves food around the mouth as the lips do, plus the tongue helps create a bolus of food to be more easily swallowed. Also, the tongue transports the food bolus backward to the pharynx where it can be moved into the esophagus. It is not unusual for a stroke to impair the tongue's mobility. Swallowing exercises (D) obviously are indicated for swallowing difficulty, especially when this is the result of a stroke.

131. B: Theories of phonological acquisition termed *Universalist-Linguistic* maintain that children acquire phonological concepts as passive learners rather than actively (D). They also hold that phonological abilities do progress in a linear fashion (A); that all children universally develop phonological knowledge in the same way, without individual differences (C). The three incorrect choices all represent principles of cognitive theories of phonological acquisition.

132. C: The first thing you should do as the SLP assessing a child for speech fluency is to screen the child's hearing and vision. Hearing or vision deficits can have impacts on all speech and language problems, including stuttering. If such deficits are not diagnosed and addressed, speech therapy for dysfluencies will be ineffective. Obtaining family and developmental history (D) from the parents should come next. After gathering information from educators and care providers and reviewing school records for children in school and preschool, the next step is to conduct an oral–peripheral examination (A) to rule in or out any abnormalities that could contribute to dysfluency. Only then can you take measures of fluency, which will in turn inform your completion of a fluency severity rating scale (B).

Practice Test #2

1. Which of the following is MOST accurate about the articulation of individuals with hearing loss who speak?

a. They must rely entirely on visual information.
b. They produce devocalized sounds more easily.
c. Vocalized speech sounds are easier to learn.
d. Voiced and unvoiced sounds are equally hard.

2. What are school-wide positive behavioral support programs MOST characterized by?

a. Intensive behavioral intervention at the lowest tiers
b. A stringent behavior modification system at all tiers
c. A greater emphasis on prevention than intervention
d. Giving positive reinforcement but never punishment

3. The following audiogram MOST represents which of the following?

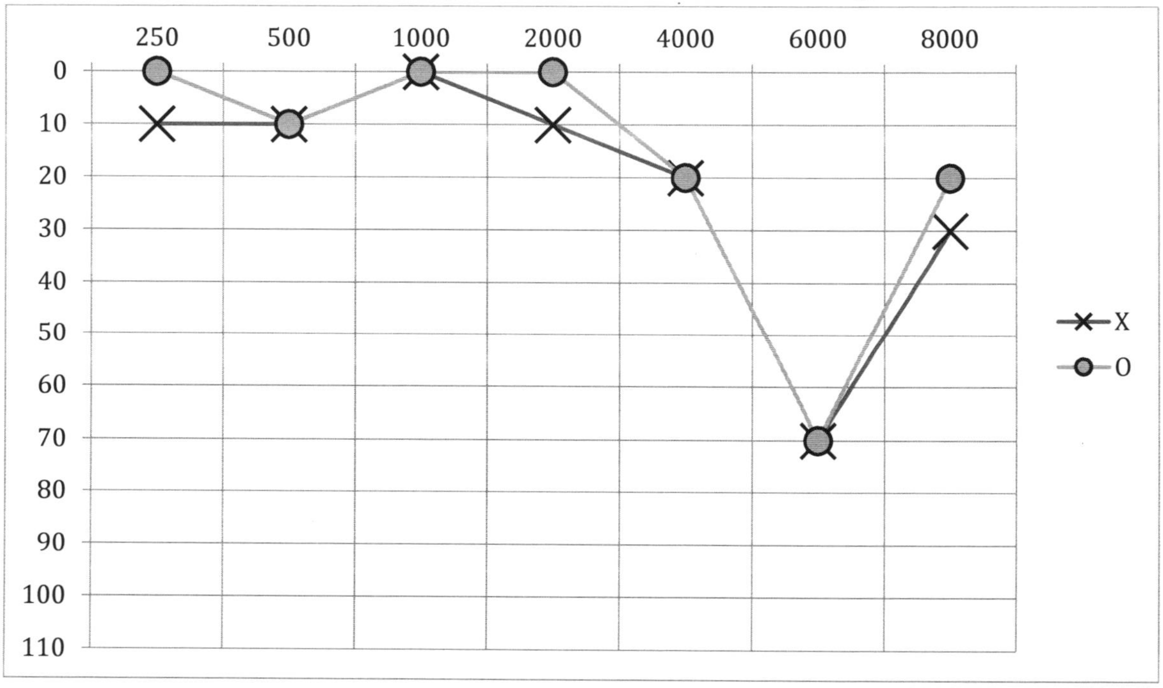

a. A left-ear conductive hearing loss
b. Bilateral age-related hearing loss
c. The hearing loss induced by noise
d. A mild sensorineural hearing loss

4. Who described the Acquisition-Learning, Monitor, Natural Order, Input, and Affective Filter hypotheses?

a. Swain
b. Cummins
c. Gregory
d. Krashen

5. Who of the following speech-language pathologists is/was NOT a specialist in the field of stuttering?

a. George H. Shames
b. Charles G. Van Riper
c. Martin F. Schwartz
d. Daniel R. Boone

6. To help educators and other professionals work with the families of children with disabilities, researchers have proposed aspects of family systems and dynamics to consider. For example, one is the way family members interact on a daily basis. Which is not another one of these aspects?

a. What resources are available to a given family
b. The nature and severity of the child's disability
c. The various individual needs of family members
d. Changes over time that affect family members

7. Hearing screening is recommended for which newborn infants?

a. Babies at risk of hearing loss
b. Every single baby who is born
c. Only babies in neonatal ICUs
d. None as it is too early to screen

8. After total laryngectomy, some patients may use a device called an HME. This is:

a. Used to prosthetically produce a voice tone
b. Used to protect the airway for respiration
c. Used to electromechanically produce voice
d. Used to highlight, mitigate, and evaluate any respiratory insufficiencies

9. The study of sentence structure and word order is called:

a. Syntax
b. Semantics
c. Pragmatics
d. Morphology

10. Ms. Wright, a speech-language pathologist, sees Tommy, a first grader, for therapy sessions focusing on his delayed language development. Tommy has a diagnosis of a seizure disorder and takes anticonvulsant medications for this. Ms. Wright has observed that, in the past three sessions, Tommy appeared inattentive, his eyelids were drooping, and she had to prompt him often to get him to attend to what she was saying. What is the most likely explanation for this?

a. Tommy is bored with the therapy sessions.
b. Tommy is not getting a good night's sleep at home.
c. Tommy is sleepy due to his anti-seizure medications.
d. Tommy is behaving this way to get more attention.

11. Antoine is a second-grader whom Glenda the SLP is evaluating at the beginning of the school year. His IQ and achievement tests are below average, but not profoundly so. When she tests his hearing, he initially responds normally, following the directions to raise his left or right hand when he hears a tone in his left or right ear. But after a couple of minutes he stops responding. Glenda keeps increasing the intensity of the tones but still gets no response. She tests the machine again by listening to the earphones herself and they work. She can get Antoine's attention easily by tapping him on the shoulder, standing in front of him, or talking to him, and he understands and answers questions. Even stranger, his teacher also reports he seems to hear and understand what is said to him. Glenda runs into her predecessor in the SLP position, who was promoted and still visits the school as part of her new job. She reports having the exact same experience with Antoine last year. So does the audiologist when she makes her periodic visit. While the school team will need neurological/psychological/psychiatric consultations for this phenomenon, which of the following is the most likely explanation for it?

a. Antoine is faking a hearing loss to receive special education or attention.
b. Antoine is suffering from conversion hysteria or psychogenic deafness.
c. Antoine is demonstrating the classic symptoms of organic hearing loss.
d. Antoine is likely to have some attentional or neurological deficiencies.

12. What is true about pre-production activities that teachers can use to encourage English-language speech by ELL students?

a. Narrating students' actions will simply make them self-conscious.
b. The activities that teachers use should involve hands-on learning.
c. It is more important that activities use speech than have meaning.
d. Language functions are irrelevant if students complete the lesson.

13. When interpreting data from a meta-analysis of multiple studies investigating interventions for stuttering, which of the following statements is MOST accurate?

a. If one study finds an intervention has small or statistically nonsignificant effects, that intervention should be discarded.
b. If one study finds an intervention has large or statistically significant effects, that intervention should be adopted.
c. With differing research methodology and confounding variables, one study sometimes suffices, or several are needed.
d. Just as diagnoses require multiple assessments, adopting an intervention requires the findings of multiple investigations.

14. An approach to language learning that begins with practical communicative usage and that over time incorporates grammar, vocabulary, phonemic awareness, etc. is known as a(n) ______approach.

a. top-down
b. functional
c. total physical response
d. natural

15. In addition to voice evaluation by an SLP and an otolaryngologist, which examination is MOST instrumental for diagnosing vocal cord paralysis?

a. An intra-oral exam
b. A perceptual exam
c. An endoscopic exam
d. None of these exams

16. What is an example of the phonemic awareness instructional strategy of keyword substitution?

a. "Show, show, show your shoat, shently..."
b. "How much is that window in the doggie"
c. "'Twas brillig, and the slithy toves / Did..."
d. "Owe, owe, owe our oat, ently own the..."

17. Emotionally, LD students are more likely to suffer from low self-esteem. Due to unsuccessful scholastic experiences, they are more likely to drop out of school. Which of these is another emotional and social consequence secondary to LD?

a. Greater risk of substance abuse
b. Greater risk of criminal actions
c. Greater risk of suicidal actions
d. Greater risks of all of these

18. In the anatomy and physiology of speech mechanisms, which structure is NOT a part of the upper air passageway?

a. The oral cavity
b. The pharynx
c. The larynx
d. The trachea

19. According to state EHDI (early hearing detection and intervention) coordinators, various gaps in the system cause many newborns failing hearing screenings to be lost to follow-up diagnosis and treatment. Which of the following is true about some of these gaps?

a. Inadequate insurance reimbursements for diagnosis often interfere with infant services.
b. Privacy regulations protect families and are not found to present obstacles to follow-up.
c. Many families are located far from EHDI facilities but still manage to pursue follow-up.
d. Follow-up for at-risk babies is lacking, but EHDI programs screen far more preschoolers.

20. In audiology, what does MCL stand for?

a. Maximum Comfort Level
b. Minimum Clarity Locutions
c. Medial Cochlear Ligaments
d. Most Comfortable Loudness

21. Which component of language is generally most affected by Broca's aphasia?

a. Expressive written language
b. Receptive written language
c. Expressive oral language
d. Receptive oral language

22. Among some of the critical components of good phonics lessons, which one is taught for the purpose of helping students to decode unfamiliar words?

a. Introducing sound-spellings
b. Blending phonemes into words
c. Discriminating phonemes in words
d. Reviewing to overlearn sound-spellings

23. When you make the sounds /t/, /d/, /s/, or /z/, normally your tongue is in contact with:

a. Your upper teeth.
b. Your alveolar ridge.
c. Your soft palate.
d. Your hard palate.

24. Marco's first language is Castilian Spanish. His English is fluent, but his teacher refers him to the speech-language pathologist for what she calls a "lisp." Upon testing it is found that this feature of his articulation is systematically used only in words with the letter "c" followed by a vowel. The most likely explanation is:

a. Marco's first language is influencing his second language.
b. Marco is demonstrating a systematic articulation disorder.
c. Marco has developed Broca's aphasia.
d. Marco has an undiagnosed case of CAS.

25. When a patient has apraxia of speech, where is the neurological damage causing it localized to?

a. Basal ganglia control circuit
b. Cerebellar control circuit
c. Right hemisphere
d. Left hemisphere

26. Regarding student records and information that school-based SLPs might gather and use from other agencies, which law takes precedence in determining confidentiality requirements?

a. The IDEA
b. The FERPA
c. The HIPAA
d. None of these

27. According to the ASHA Code of Ethics, which of the following can an SLP ethically do?

a. Use correspondence to deliver services to a homebound disabled client
b. Use correspondence carefully and thoroughly to deliver an SLP diagnosis
c. Use correspondence to give general educational information about SLP
d. Decline to provide professional services because of somebody's religion

28. Presbycusis is most often characterized by:

a. More hearing loss at lower frequencies
b. More hearing loss at middle frequencies
c. Uniform hearing loss at all frequencies
d. More loss at higher frequencies

29. Kenny has a phonological disorder. He pronounces his own name "Tenny." He pronounces "I gotta go" as "I dotta doe." These are examples of which place of articulation?

a. He is substituting front phonemes with back phonemes.
b. He is substituting back phonemes with front phonemes.
c. He is substituting middle phonemes with front phonemes.
d. He is substituting back phonemes with middle phonemes.

30. Among theories of language acquisition, which idea is MOST compatible with the observation that children develop language in similar patterns across various cultural contexts?

a. B. F. Skinner's environmental influence
b. Whorf's linguistic relativity hypothesis
c. Noam Chomsky's biological influences
d. Neural networks theories of language

31. Which assistive technology is most appropriate for a student with a voice disorder that interferes with audible speech production?

a. Speech-to-text computer software
b. Text-to-speech computer software
c. Voice recognition computer software
d. Voice synthesizer computer software

32. Research has found that in elementary school-age children, working memory:

a. Increases with age
b. Decreases with age
c. Stays stable with age
d. Fluctuates over time

33. Of the following cranial nerves, which does NOT have sensory functions?

a. I
b. II
c. VIII
d. VI

34. Within all world languages, which word order is used by the largest number of people?

a. Subject-Object-Verb (SOV)
b. Verb-Subject-Object (VSO)
c. Verb-Object-Subject (VOS)
d. Subject-Verb-Object (SVO)

35. A teacher initiates a guessing game to promote phonological awareness with first graders. The teacher presents picture cards and speaks each word depicted very slowly (e.g., "sssssuuuuunnnnn") to emphasize its phonemes, and children must guess the words. Which phonological process does this teach?

a. Blending phonemes
b. Deleting phonemes
c. Segmenting phonemes
d. Substituting phonemes

36. You have a software program that analyzes test instruments for reliability. You use it to see how well the items on a norm-referenced test correlate with each other. This measure is an example of which type of reliability?

a. Test-retest reliability
b. Parallel forms reliability
c. Decision consistency reliability
d. Internal consistency reliability

37. Due to his disabilities, it takes Donald years to learn to say one word. His therapists have most likely found which technique most effective when working on speech?

a. Only reinforcing his eventual correct utterance of the target word
b. Reinforcing all attempts, as it is so hard for him to produce a word
c. Differentially reinforcing attempts and successive approximations
d. Always similarly reinforcing both attempts and successive approximations

38. What will a person with profound bilateral sensorineural hearing loss benefit MOST from?

a. Bilateral hearing aids
b. Cochlear implant(s)
c. Both A and B.
d. Neither A nor B

39. Among serious complications of dysphagia, which of these is MOST related to aspiration of liquids?

a. Dehydration
b. Malnutrition
c. Pneumonias
d. Asphyxiation

40. How many muscles and nerves does the normal adult human process of eating and swallowing involve?

a. More than 40
b. Fewer than 20
c. More than 30
d. Fewer than 10

41. Christopher is a student with concerns in the area of academics who scored in the below-average range on an academic achievement test. Which of the following disability categories would Christopher most likely be eligible for?

a. Speech or language impairment
b. Other health impairment
c. Specific learning disability
d. Cognitive disability

42. Which of the following has most recently been determined to be the most important factor in Piaget's cognitive development theory?

a. Nature
b. Nurture
c. Learning processes
d. Inherent structures

43. To teach students nonverbal communication skills, what have some teachers discovered through experience?

a. Nonverbal communication should be taught to students in large portions.
b. Nonverbal communication should be taught using appropriate situations.
c. Nonverbal communication does not require students to have confidence.
d. Nonverbal communication does not involve creativity from the students.

44. When screening children for autism spectrum disorders (ASDs) specifically, which characteristic of the screening tool is MOST likely to be the LEAST realistic or diagnostic?

a. Sensitivity
b. Specificity
c. Positive predictive value
d. Negative predictive value

45. What is NOT true about nasal emission?

a. It is a type of nasal resonance problem.
b. It can often accompany hypernasality.
c. It can be due to palatal insufficiency.
d. It rarely exists for functional reasons.

46. On a continuum, which of these represents the most complex level of phonological awareness?

a. Segmenting words into their individual syllables and blending individual syllables into words
b. Phonemic awareness, i.e., understanding words consist of phonemes and manipulating these
c. Segmenting words into their onsets and rimes and blending onsets and rimes into full words
d. Segmenting sentences, i.e., understanding speech consists of separate words, and rhyming songs

47. Samuel is a student with a specific learning disability in the area of oral expression. What kind of assessment would be most appropriate in order to evaluate his continued eligibility?

a. Expressive language
b. Receptive language
c. Auditory discrimination
d. Verbal intelligence

48. When parents have a baby with profound hearing loss and are trying to decide whether to use ASL (American Sign Language) or hearing aids until the baby is of the age recommended for cochlear implants, which of these is most accurate about the role of the SLP?

a. Counseling parents about ASL should only be by a deaf educator.
b. Only the surgeon to do cochlear implantation should advise them.
c. It is within the scope of the SLP to counsel parents on this decision.
d. Only the audiologist should counsel the parents about hearing aids.

49. Of the following principles for treating language disorders, which is MOST appropriate for infants, toddlers, and preschoolers?

a. Promoting social interaction
b. Increasing functional flexibility
c. Slower treatment than in school
d. The least restrictive environment

50. Which of the following is/are MOST important for selecting norm-referenced tests for evaluating language skills in preschool (ages 4 and 5 years) children?

a. Use psychometric review to find tests meeting the majority of criteria
b. Use both psychometric review plus data-based validation procedures
c. Use data-based validation procedures instead of psychometric review
d. Use psychometric review to find tests with high inter-rater reliability

51. Which of the following is true about children who begin formal school with language deficits?

a. Family preferences of news and current affairs over literature cause language deficiencies.
b. Children's deficiencies in language development can compromise their social relationships.
c. Assessment has revealed that most children with language deficits have lower intelligence.
d. Children's language development is not influenced by peers' relative valuations of reading.

52. Among exercises to improve swallowing ability in cases of dysphagia, not all involve actually swallowing. One of these is the Shaker exercise, which involves lifting the head but not the shoulders while lying flat on the back. Which of the following is another swallowing exercise that does NOT involve swallowing?

a. The Mendelsohn maneuver
b. The hyoid lift maneuver
c. The effortful swallow
d. The supraglottic swallow

53. In the anatomy and physiology of the hearing mechanisms, where are the ossicles located?

a. Pinna
b. Middle ear
c. Ear canal
d. Inner ear

54. Which of the following is true in regards to stuttering?

a. Three genes attributed to stuttering have been identified.
b. All stuttering is genetic in nature.
c. Developmental stuttering is not found to run in families.
d. Familial stuttering is attributed to environmental factors.

55. Among students with specific language impairment (SLI), those with prognoses of the least cognitive, educational, and social difficulties are those whose problems are mostly with:

a. Syntax
b. Prosody
c. Phonology
d. Semantics

56. The neurological damage is localized to the cerebellar control circuit in which type of dysarthria?

a. Flaccid
b. Spastic
c. Ataxic
d. Hypokinetic

57. Which test assesses knowledge of the meaning of both English and Spanish words?

a. TOLD: Picture Vocabulary subtest
b. Peabody Picture Vocabulary Test
c. Toronto Tests of Receptive Vocabulary
d. Assessment of Children's Language Comprehension test

58. What percent of all speech problems are attributed to various degrees of hearing loss?

a. More than 50 percent
b. Fewer than 5 percent
c. More than 10 percent
d. Fewer than 8 percent

59. The study of speech perception has determined that the phonemes produced in human speech:

a. are linear or sequential in their production.
b. are invariant in waveform representations.
c. are influenced and varied by co-articulation.
d. are heard on a continuum as colors are seen.

60. Which of these semantic intervention tasks is most similar to Sentence Completion?

a. Cloze format
b. Using riddles
c. 20 Questions
d. Role playing

61. Which of the following is unlikely to be observed in a preschool-aged child with delayed phonological development?

a. Delayed morphological development
b. Delayed syntactic development
c. Delayed discourse structure development
d. Delayed muscular development

62. What is the only unpaired muscle in the larynx?

a. Cricothyroid
b. Oblique arytenoid
c. Transverse arytenoid
d. Superior thyroarytenoid

63. Dr. Murray Bowen's Family Systems Theory posits four basic relationship patterns. One of these is "Impairment of one or more children." Which is not a characteristic of this pattern?

a. Excessive parental worry about the child
b. Having an overly idealized view of the child
c. Less reaction by the child to parental focus
d. Having an overly negative view of the child

64. Which of these conditions include(s) *consistent, overall* hypernasality of voice as a characteristic?

a. Dysarthrias
b. Cleft palate
c. Speech apraxia
d. (A) and (B)

65. For someone with velopharyngeal incompetence due to dysarthria, which of these prosthetic devices would be indicated?

a. A palatal lift
b. A palatal obturator
c. A speech bulb obturator
d. None of these

66. For testing neurological disorders affecting speech and language, which instrumental technology can *noninvasively* show the relative *metabolic* activity levels of various parts of the brain?

a. fMRI
b. MRI
c. EEG
d. PET

67. Clara has a diagnosis of Wernicke's aphasia. What is NOT true about this disorder?

a. Clara can speak fluently but cannot understand what others say.
b. Clara's speech makes sense but will deteriorate without feedback.
c. Clara's words all have meaning but are not arranged in proper order.
d. Clara will probably develop compensatory strategies like stock phrases.

68. According to ASHA, which of the following is true of ethical behavior by a supervising SLP?

a. It is the responsibility of the supervisee to keep from violating the ASHA Code of Ethics.
b. It is the supervisor's responsibility to keep supervisees from violating the Code of Ethics.
c. If a supervisor delegates service tasks, delegated staff are responsible for client welfare.
d. It is acceptable if supervisors delegate professional tasks to nonprofessional supervisees.

69. Which of the following is included among indirect therapeutic approaches to stuttering?

a. Modeling a decreased rate of speaking
b. Targeting pragmatics in everyday speech
c. Practicing relaxed breathing techniques
d. Not interrupting the stutterer's utterance

70. As an SLP, you implement the first stuttering therapy program for a client. After collecting data for three months, you find that measures of the client's stuttering levels, while inconsistent, always reflect less than 20 percent improvement. What does this mean?

a. These results show no more improvement than could have occurred by chance.
b. These results show that the client is making adequate albeit slow improvement.
c. These results show your measurements are inaccurate and need to be changed.
d. These results show your therapy is ineffective and must be discarded or replaced.

71. Of the following, which symptom(s) is/are LEAST associated with cognitive communication disorders?

a. Impaired language content and form and impaired speech
b. Impaired ability to participate in interactive conversations
c. Impaired ability to interpret and express verbal pragmatics
d. Impaired executive functions like planning or problem-solving

72. Stuttering involves disorders with all of these EXCEPT?

a. Rate
b. Rhythm
c. Fluency
d. Volume

73. Echolalia is:

a. Repeating oneself over and over
b. Repeating what other people say
c. Hearing echoes when others speak
d. The inability to control the volume of one's speech

74. Of the following theories, concepts, and models of stuttering, which one is the MOST recent?

a. Cerebral dominance theory
b. Covert repair hypothesis
c. Psychological theory
d. Diagnostic theory

75. For patients having Amyotrophic Lateral Sclerosis (ALS), which of the following represents the MOST severe level of swallowing difficulty on the ALS Severity Scale?

a. The patient aspirates secretions instead of swallowing them.
b. Medications and/or suction are used to manage secretions.
c. The patient requires tube feedings as supplements to eating.
d. The patient requires tube feedings with nothing given orally.

76. Which of the following words contains consonant digraphs but no consonant blends?

a. Shocking
b. Screams
c. Splashes
d. Smoking

77. Which is true about nasal air emission and its effects on speech and/or resonance?

a. Its unobstructed form affects intra-oral breath pressure.
b. Its obstructed form influences intra-oral breath pressure.
c. Unobstructed and obstructed forms affect oral pressure.
d. Both forms occur during the production of vowel sounds.

78. Which of the following behavioral or emotional disorders is MOST likely to coexist with a phonological disorder?

a. School phobia
b. Depression
c. Anxiety
d. ADHD

79. Between four and six months of age, what is a typical expressive language characteristic of normally developing babies?

a. Babbling and vocal play
b. Differentiation of cries
c. Smiling, cooing, and gooing
d. Saying their first words

80. A "notch" audiogram (sometimes called "cookie-bite") with a sharp dip in acuity around 4,000 Hz typically represents what kind of hearing?

a. A normal curve of hearing
b. Noise-induced hearing loss
c. Conductive hearing losses
d. Age-related hearing losses

81. Which of the following causes of dysphagia is classified as a neurological disorder?

a. Thyromegaly
b. Polymyositis
c. Poliomyelitis
d. A neoplasm

82. Which method of treatment for language disorders is found to be especially effective with children from socially disadvantaged backgrounds?

a. Self-talk
b. Modeling
c. Cognitive
d. Behavioral

83. Tympanometry is an acoustic test designed to assess the condition of which portion of the ear?

a. Outer
b. Inner
c. Middle
d. Auditory nerve

84. Which of the following is NOT a psychogenic voice disorder?

a. Conversion muteness
b. Spasmodic dysphonia
c. Conversion aphonia
d. Mutational falsetto

85. What is the MOST frequent etiology of aphasia in adults?

a. Dementia
b. Stroke
c. Illness
d. TBI

86. Which statement is correct about how teachers can model appropriate listening and speaking behaviors for students?

a. Teachers can model these when they facilitate book discussions, not in everyday conversations.
b. Teachers can model these better when giving whole-class instruction rather than small-group teaching.
c. Teachers can model these more authentically in one-to-one conversations than in discussions of media.
d. Teachers can model these and support them by thinking aloud about specific content they teach.

87. Regarding referrals, which of the following actions by the SLP would be acceptable in view of the ASHA Code of Ethics?

a. To refer a client to another professional or agency based on the client's best interest
b. To refer a client to another professional or agency based on the SLP's financial interest
c. To refer a client to another professional or agency based on the SLP's personal interest
d. To give a client services based only on a referral from a personal or professional source

88. When assessing error patterns in a student's reading, which is most detrimental to reading proficiency?

a. Substitution of "control" for "contrariness"
b. Substitution of "resistant" for "recalcitrant"
c. Substituting a noun, not a verb, for a noun
d. Substituting for errors informed by context

89. In which stage of language development is a child who says "I can't tomorrow" and "It's behind you"?

a. The three-word stage
b. Complex utterances
c. The four-word stage
d. Cannot be discerned

90. If a dysphagia patient is found to have some esophageal obstruction, which of the following treatment options would be indicated?

a. Dilation and/or medication
b. Endoscopy and/or surgery
c. Exercises and/or medication
d. Diet change and/or exercises

91. Which of these is a motor speech disorder that causes difficulty in the brain's programming and planning of motor movements?

a. Apraxia
b. Ataxia
c. Anoxia
d. Hypoxia

92. Anya's parents do not speak English. Which is the best strategy for the school to communicate her assessment results to them?

a. Tell them to Anya and ask her to tell her parents
b. Arrange for an interpreter to attend the meeting
c. Send them a report translated into their language
d. Excuse the parents, and just get their IEP signature

93. Among specific components of reading difficulties, which category is a result of the other two?

a. Difficulties with decoding words
b. Difficulties with comprehending
c. Difficulties with retention of text
d. Difficulties with all are unrelated

94. Which of the following has not been reported by families as a result of having children with disabilities?

a. Experiencing more stress in the family
b. An improvement in family dynamics
c. Focusing on the child's positive attributes
d. All of these have been reported by families

95. For whom is an IEP legally required to provide treatment for language disorders?

a. Preschoolers and school-age children
b. Infants, toddlers, and preschoolers
c. Toddlers and preschoolers only
d. School-age children only

96. Which of the following are MOST often caused by vocal abuse or misuse?

a. Vocal cord polyps
b. Vocal cord nodules
c. Neither one of these
d. Both of these equally

97. Jane has cerebral palsy characterized by poor balance, lack of muscle tone, and a slight reoccurring tremor. Which type of cerebral palsy does Jane have?

a. Diplegic
b. Ataxic
c. Dyskinetic
d. Spastic

98. In second language acquisition, what is Stage II also called?

a. Speech Emergence Stage
b. Receptive Stage
c. Intermediate Proficiency Stage
d. Early Production Stage

99. Children with genetically based linguistic processing deficits that affect their speech are:

a. among the majority of those referred to SLPs for help with their speech.
b. among the minority of those referred to SLPs for help with their speech.
c. among a smaller group than those having genetic speech motor deficits.
d. among a smaller group than those with conductive hearing loss etiology.

100. According to the experience of SLP ASHA members and other experts, which of the following is accurate about using computer technology to reduce the time school SLPs spent on paperwork?

a. SLPs can use computers for office work, but using them at IEP meetings is only a distraction.
b. School systems frown on using e-mail to correspond with parents, teachers, administrators.
c. You should avoid computerizing a master goal list because student needs are individualized.
d. For students moving within state, uniform statewide forms reduce time learning their IEPs.

101. The International Phonetic Alphabet symbol /ʃ/ represents the initial consonant sound in:

a. "Sass"
b. "Foe"
c. "Cha"
d. "She"

102. Of the following measures made in a speech fluency assessment, which one is the MOST subjective?

a. Stuttering frequency
b. Stuttering duration
c. Speech naturalness
d. Rate of speech

103. Regarding cases of congenital deafness and hearing loss, which of these is correct?

a. More than half of these cases are caused by environmental factors.
b. The majority of cases of genetic deafness are not due to syndromes.
c. More cases of genetic deafness are secondary to genetic syndromes.
d. Syndromic and nonsyndromic deafness are always genetic in origin.

104. Which of the following treatments is NOT used for denasality?

a. Ear training
b. Target voice models
c. Establishing new pitch
d. Explanation of problem

105. A kindergarten teacher has received a community outreach referral. She asks the school's speech-language pathologist to evaluate a preschool child for delayed language development, as the parents cannot afford to pay a private practitioner's fees. The parents bring their child to the school. The speech-language pathologist assesses the child and privately has a strong suspicion that this child is displaying many signs of early autism. The speech-language pathologist takes the appropriate action. What does she do?

a. Tells the parents what she suspects and recommends treatment
b. Refers the parents to a free community clinic for a complete behavioral assessment
c. Asks the referring kindergarten teacher to tell the parents that she suspects autism
d. Recommends that the parents take their child to their pediatrician for a checkup

106. Which is true about *dynamic assessments* or diagnostic interventions in SLP?

a. These can help test children with ASDs, ID, and other developmental disabilities.
b. These are very similar to standardized, norm-referenced assessment instruments.
c. These are unlikely to use observations of the child's spontaneous communication.
d. These are likely to take less time to administer than standardized test instruments.

107. Of the following statements, which one reflects the genetic principle of independent assortment?

a. One allele from each parent's pair of alleles for a trait passes to the offspring.
b. The process of meiosis that forms sex cells affects the inheritance of alleles.
c. The genes for certain inherited traits are located on different chromosomes.
d. Inheriting a particular trait does not influence inheritance of a different trait.

108. Speech featuring mixed nasality is characterized by:

a. Hypernasality when producing oral vowels and hyponasality of nasal consonants.
b. Hypernasality/nasal air emission on oral consonants and hyponasal nasal consonants.
c. Hypernasality/nasal air emission on nasal vowels and hyponasal oral consonants.
d. Hypernasality/nasal air emission on nasal consonants and hyponasal oral vowels.

109. Dysarthria is:

a. A neurologically caused articulation disorder
b. A learning disability affecting reading ability
c. A neurologically caused swallowing disorder
d. An articulation disorder of the speech organs

110. A patient has developed dysphagia, and the cause is found to be iatrogenic. Which of the following etiologies would LEAST fit this diagnosis?

a. Caustic materials
b. Surgical resection
c. Radiation fibrosis
d. Drug side effects

111. Patients with neurological damage to (the) _____ hemisphere are more likely to have other problems in addition to difficulties with their language and speech.

a. Left
b. Right
c. Either
d. Neither

112. Of the following syndromes that can affect speech-language development, which one is classified as a metabolic disorder?

a. Turner syndrome
b. Hunter syndrome
c. DiGeorge syndrome
d. Klinefelter syndrome

113. A phonological disorder is a language disorder that affects the _______ level, entailing cognitive functions that organize speech sounds into contrasting patterns.

a. Phonemic
b. Phonetic
c. Syntactic
d. Linguistic

114. What is NOT a characteristic or tendency that would cause difficulty with semantics?

a. Concrete thinking
b. Limited imagery
c. Divergent thinking
d. Narrow perception

115. Tommy is 9 years old and has a vocabulary of about 1,000 words, can count up to seven things, and speaks in simple sentences. What is this description MOST typical of?

a. Delayed development
b. Normal development
c. A language disorder
d. Intellectual disability

116. An upper-level elementary school teacher is developing a unit on American history. How can he use formative assessments to support his students' English language and literacy development?

a. Create versions of the unit test to support learners with different linguistic needs.
b. Have English learners complete an alternative project that does not require essay writing such as a visual display of American history.
c. Administer a unit-end assessment to determine mastery.
d. Conduct informal checks on the daily language objective of the lesson, so the teacher can incorporate his observations into the next day's lesson.

117. Researchers conduct a meta-analysis of the findings of multiple studies investigating an intervention for stuttering. All studies included random group assignment of participants. With a 95% confidence interval, they find the intervention has an effect size of .854, with a lower limit of .507 and an upper limit of 1.202. Based on these data, which of the following is correct?

a. Whether the effects were statistically significant is unknown with only these data.
b. A causal relationship between the intervention and the effects can be confirmed.
c. The average effect of this intervention was, at worst, none and, at best, moderate.
d. The average effect of the intervention equals the effect for every individual study.

118. Perry has difficulties with differentiating among printed characters and with getting things in the correct order. These would be classified as:

a. A perceptual disorder
b. A reasoning disorder
c. A memory disorder
d. None of these

119. Which of the following do Huntington disease, Parkinson disease, Wilson disease, and multiple sclerosis all have in common?

a. All are progressive diseases wherein both motor control problems and dementia are possible or likely.
b. All are degenerative diseases wherein both motor control problems and dementia always exist.
C. All are progressive diseases wherein dementia exists and motor control problems are possible or likely.
d. All are degenerative diseases wherein motor control problems exist and dementia is possible or likely.

120. Cheryl is African-American. She and her parents regularly substitute /d/ for /ð/, for example, "I can do dis." What is this?

a. A developmental disorder they share
b. A phonological feature of their dialect
c. A kind of phonological process disorder
d. A kind of functional articulation disorder

121. An IFSP is required by law for treating a language disorder in:

a. a school-age child.
b. an infant or a toddler.
c. a toddler or preschooler.
d. a preschool or school-age child.

122. The original three-stage model normal eating and swallowing physiology was expanded to a four-stage model. Which of the following correctly represents the additional stage?

a. The pharyngeal stage was divided into two stages.
b. The oral stage was subdivided into two stages.
c. The esophageal stage was divided into two stages.
d. The additional fourth epigastric stage was added.

123. Students in a third-grade intermediate-level English Language Development (ELD) class are developing their classroom presentation registers. Which activity would best help them?

a. Writing out their presentations on index cards
b. Practicing pronouncing different key vocabulary words for the presentation
c. Explicit teaching and modeling of how to deliver a class presentation
d. Editing each other's work and slides for grammatical errors

124. A seventh-grade science teacher with several beginning-level English learners in his class considers how he can modify his speech to best support his learners. Which is NOT an effective modification of his speech?

a. Repeating key words
b. Using the primary language for directions
c. Simplifying the syntax of a sentence
d. Increasing his talk time for explanations

125. You meet a post-CVA patient who says things to you such as, "My, don't you look pretty today," "What a nice dress," and "Do you think it will rain this afternoon?" However, she does not directly answer your questions. When you point at her watch, she says, "Looking at it, looking at it . . ." and engages in long, rambling discourses. What is she MOST likely to have?

a. Wernicke's aphasia
b. Broca's aphasia
c. Global aphasia
d. No aphasia

126. Of the following resonance dysfunctions, which is characterized by a muffled quality, sometimes described as "potato in the mouth speech"?

a. Cul-de-Sac resonance
b. Hypernasal resonance
c. Hyponasal resonance
d. Absence of resonance

127. Researchers have identified which of the following about norm-referenced reading tests?

a. They are better for assessing abstract cognitive levels.
b. They are better for assessing in homogeneous groups.
c. They are better for assessing narrow ranges of ability.
d. They are better for assessing limited outcome ranges.

128. Mrs. Stroud's pupil Janet has delayed language development and reading difficulties. Mrs. Stroud discovers that Janet's mother does not help her with reading at home. It turns out that Janet's mother is not unwilling; rather, she lacks confidence in her own reading skills and has been embarrassed to admit this. How can Mrs. Stroud help in this situation?

a. Refer Janet's mother to a reading teacher for free adult education sessions in the community and have a few group practice sessions with Janet, her mother, and both teachers.
b. Schedule private sessions herself with Janet's mother to improve her reading skills and teach her how to help Janet at home with her reading and her homework.
c. Schedule more time with Janet to work on her reading skills and assignments, since her mother is not able to help Janet at home with reading-related activities.
d. Arrange for a tutor to make home visits to work with Janet on her reading assignments, since her mother does not have the necessary reading skills to do this.

129. In the swallowing process, which two cranial nerves each control the largest number of muscles involved?

a. Trigeminal (V) and Facial (VII)
b. Glossopharyngeal (IX) and Vagus (X)
c. Vagus (X) and Hypoglossal (XII)
d. Facial (VII) and Glossopharyngeal (IX)

130. In an unfamiliar word encountered while reading, a student does not recognize the first part of the word, but does recognize that it ends in *-tion,* meaning it is a noun and the first part probably derives from a verb. Which term best describes the syllable *-tion*?

a. A phoneme
b. A morpheme
c. A grapheme
d. A sememe

131. Of the following, which statement is MOST accurate regarding counseling clients as part of the SLP's clinical practice?

a. Most SLPs feel counseling is not their role even though their degree programs included counseling courses.
b. Most SLPs did not receive counseling courses in their degree programs and feel counseling is not in their roles.
c. Most SLPs feel counseling is within their role but received no counseling courses in their degree programs.
d. Most SLPs have received counseling courses in their degree programs and feel counseling is within their roles.

132. "By next week, we *will have completed* all four reports." The italicized part of the previous sentence is an example of which grammatical category?

a. Person
b. Case
c. Tense
d. Number

Answer Key and Explanations for Test #2

1. C: Deaf and hard-of-hearing (HOH) individuals can learn to produce vocalized (voiced) speech sounds more easily because even the deaf can feel the vibrations, and the hard-of-hearing can hear some of the sound. Hence, they rely not only on visual information (A) but also on vibrations and residual hearing in those who have it. Devocalized (unvoiced) sounds are harder, not easier, to learn (C) for those with hearing loss because the HOH have less information without sound and the deaf have less information without vocal vibration. Thus, (D) is incorrect. The most successful speakers having hearing loss use a combination of all information available (auditory/sound, tactile/vibration, and visual/speech reading).

2. C: Positive behavioral support programs emphasize prevention by giving all students positive reinforcement and other supports for desired behaviors. These are found to avert many behavior problems at the lower tiers, thus (A) is incorrect. Educators introduce intervention as needed in the middle tier(s) and provide progressively more intensive intervention to the highest tier, thus (B) is incorrect. It is not true that such programs eschew punishment (D): This and other aversive consequences for undesirable behaviors may be introduced as well as using positive reinforcement for desirable behaviors.

3. C: The audiogram pictured shows normal hearing at the low and middle frequencies, with a sharp drop in hearing acuity at the upper middle frequencies. This so-called "noise notch" audiogram is typical of noise-induced hearing loss. The loss is bilateral, not left-ear (A) only. An audiogram for age-related hearing loss (B) or presbycusis typically shows a more gradual slope, with the least hearing loss at the lower frequencies, increasing to the greatest hearing loss at the highest frequencies. At the frequencies where there is hearing loss, it is NOT mild (D) but rather moderate to severe (60–70 dB).

4. D: Krashen. Acquisition-Learning, Monitor, Natural Order, Input, and Affective Filter hypotheses are central to Steven Krashen's highly respected theory of second language acquisition. Language Acquisition is subconscious and requires meaningful communication, while Language Learning is conscious and involves formal instruction; the Monitor is concerned with editing and correcting errors in speaking or writing; Natural Order finds there is a predictable natural order in which grammatical structures are absorbed; Input refers to the hypothesis that language is ultimately acquired and not learned, and the Affective Filter hypothesis explores ways in which positive and negative factors such as motivation, self-esteem, and anxiety help or hurt the acquisition of language.

5. D: Daniel R. Boone (D) of the University of Arizona specializes in voice disorders and voice therapy, not stuttering. George H. Shames (A), professor emeritus of the University of Pittsburgh, was director of the university's speech clinic for 40 years and a licensed clinical psychologist, and specialized in stuttering. He developed "Stutter-Free Speech" and invented three biofeedback devices for stuttering. Shames was influenced by Charles G. Van Riper (B), a lifelong severe stutterer himself, who founded the speech clinic at Western Michigan State Normal School in Kalamazoo, and was the first chair of the school's speech pathology and audiology department. Martin F. Schwartz (C) from NYU Medical Center was a researcher in cleft lip and cleft palate surgery who stumbled on neck constriction in stutterers in 1974. Schwartz had been using ultrasound imaging on stutterers and found they had laryngeal spasms, ultimately discovering that the physical origin of stuttering was a reflexive locking of the vocal cords. He then created the passive-inhalation airflow technique of stuttering therapy. He directs the National Center for Stuttering.

6. B: The nature and severity of the child's disability (b) is certainly a factor that must be considered, but it is not itself an aspect of family systems or family dynamics. Aspects of family systems and dynamics that professionals should consider to work more effectively with families of children with disabilities include (a) what resources an individual family has at its disposal, (c) the different individual needs of various members of each family, and (d) changes that occur over time and have impacts on the members of the family.

7. B: Universal newborn hearing screening is advised by ASHA and other organizations concerned with health. Hearing loss is the most common newborn disability and has often gone undetected without newborn hearing screening. Early intervention (which depends on early detection) is found to prevent or minimize language development and learning problems due to hearing loss. The recommendation for hearing screening is not limited to babies at higher risk for hearing loss (A), such as infants in neonatal intensive care units (C), who must be screened, but encompasses all newborns. Following birth is NOT too early to screen (D) for hearing problems.

8. B: The HME device is (B) used to protect the airway for respiration. HME stands for Heat and Moisture Exchanger. It is a filter installed to the tracheostoma which captures heat and moisture from the air exhaled through it. Then, when the patient inhales, some of this captured heat and moisture are picked up so the patient is not breathing cool, dry outside air. This protects the airway. Total laryngectomy patients have lost the air moisturizing and warming functions of their noses because they now breathe through their necks via a tracheostoma instead of through the nose. This causes mucus to become more viscous, reducing escalator transport. It can also result in excessive phlegm production. The simple HME device restores some of the air conditioning and filtration. The HME is not used to produce a voice, either prosthetically (A) or electromechanically (C). It is only used to condition and filter the air inhaled by the patient. Choice (D) is an invented choice.

9. A: Sentence structure and word order and/or their study are called syntax (A). Semantics (B) refers to the study of meaning in language. Pragmatics (C) refers to the study of how context contributes to meaning. Morphology (D) refers to the study of the structure of words.

10. C: While a student who is very bored could certainly nod off, this is not the most likely explanation in the case of a child taking medications for a seizure disorder. Boredom should not be the first reason to consider. Therefore, option A is incorrect.

Whereas some children may not get a good night's sleep at home, there is no reason to assume that as the first possibility in this case. Ms. Wright has no background information that Tommy's parents let him stay up late, that he lives in an environment that is noisy at night, or that his sleep is disrupted by parents working different shifts, sharing a bedroom with an infant, or any other such factors. Therefore, option B is incorrect.

Many anti-seizure medications are known to cause drowsiness as a side effect. Different drugs can be tried, but some will not control an individual's seizures. So, some medications will make those who use them very sleepy. Therefore, option C is correct.

There is no reason to assume Tommy is deliberately acting sleepy to get more attention. He is in individual therapy sessions with Ms. Wright, has her individual attention, and has no other students with whom to compete. Whereas first graders are certainly capable of engaging in attention-seeking behavior, at this age the most likely kinds of attention-seeking behavior would not usually be pretending to fall asleep. Anti-seizure medications are a more obvious source of daytime sleepiness in a child this age. Therefore, option D is incorrect.

11. D: Antoine is likely to have some attentional or neurological deficiencies. The fact that he always starts out responding normally to the sound stimuli indicates that he can hear them, which eliminates symptoms of organic hearing loss (C). It may be that his attention wanders after a few minutes, or some neurological abnormality may cause him to cease noticing sound stimuli after a few minutes. Though malingering (A) is not impossible, it is unlikely due to Antoine's young age and the absence of complaints that he can't hear when spoken to. From interviews and other measures, Antoine also does not demonstrate the knowledge, understanding, sophistication, or initiative to try to manipulate adults or the system this way. He does not display any other attention-seeking behaviors. He is not suffering from hysterical conversion deafness (B) because he does not display any hearing loss with others' speech or other auditory stimuli, and responds normally for the first few minutes of the hearing tests. Deafness by conversion hysteria would result in a uniform failure to respond to auditory stimuli.

12. B: Experts find that narrating ELL students' actions, i.e., linguistic encoding, helps encourage them to speak English (A), that teachers should assign activities that include hands-on learning (B), and that the activities they assign should be meaningful (C). They also find that teachers should focus on which language function the students must apply to complete a lesson, not just that they complete it (D).

13. D: We do not use the results of just one assessment to make a diagnosis. Interpreting research data is analogous: We cannot choose a particular intervention approach based on the results of one research study of that intervention. Just as multiple assessments are needed for diagnosis, multiple studies are needed to judge the potential effectiveness of an intervention. One study may show statistically nonsignificant or weak effects of an intervention, while another may show significant or good effects of the same intervention. Therefore, a treatment method should neither be discarded (A) nor adopted (B) based on only one study, and the results of only one study are never sufficient (C) for this decision.

14. A: A Top-down approach to language learning begins with practical communicative usage that, over time, incorporates grammar, vocabulary, phonemic awareness, and other essential elements of speech. The top-down approach emphasizes meaningful use of language over accurate use of language elements. The functional approach also emphasizes practical use of language but emphasizes spoken language over written language, whereas the top-down method may use both written and spoken language together. Total physical response pairs physical action with learning to build solid associations with concepts. The natural approach tends to follow the pattern of first language acquisition, giving learners time to listen without speaking and slowly emerge into speech.

15. C: An endoscope provides imaging of the vocal cords and their movement or lack thereof. An intra-oral exam (A) is limited to the oral cavity; the tonsils can be seen but not the vocal cords. A perceptual exam (B) typically involves assessing a speech sample from the patient. It can be used to detect symptoms of vocal cord paralysis (e.g., weak or breathy voice, becoming winded too easily from speech, etc., which can also be symptoms of other conditions); it cannot diagnose this condition definitively as it does not include imaging as endoscopy does. Because (C) is correct, (D) is incorrect.

16. A: Keyword substitution involves replacing a phoneme in key words of song lyrics or other common phrases and sayings. This gives children practice in wordplay and is entertaining. After singing the revised lyrics, teachers can discuss with children how changing one phoneme changed the meanings of words in the song. Changing /r/ to /ʃ/ in "Row, row, row your boat" (A) is an example. Choice B transposes the two nouns in the lyric. Keyword substitution refers to substituting different phonemes in key words, not substituting different whole words or transposing existing words. Choice C quotes the first line of Lewis Carroll's poem "Jabberwocky," famous for using many nonsense words. Choice D uses the same song as choice A but deletes initial phonemes rather than substituting.

17. D: Greater risks of all of these (d) are secondary to having LDs. Individuals with LDs are at higher risk of abusing substances (a) as self-medication for the frustration, depression, anxiety, feelings of low self-worth, social isolation, and loneliness they often experience as a result of difficulties with learning and achieving in school. They are at higher risk of engaging in criminal activity (b), which is acting-out behavior in reaction against a system with which they are unable to comply successfully. Because of the depression, low self-esteem, and social isolation they often experience, LD children also have higher risks of attempting or committing suicide (c).

18. D: The trachea, also called the "windpipe," is below the larynx (C) and is not a part of the upper air passageway, which consists of the nasal cavities, the oral cavity (A), the pharynx (B), and the larynx. The trachea forks into dual bronchi that lead to the lungs.

19. A: State EHDI coordinators cite inadequate reimbursement for diagnosis as one barrier to connecting newborns who fail hearing screenings with needed services. Other obstacles they identify to follow up include privacy regulations (B), the lack of proximity for many families to EHDI facilities (C) because there are not enough facilities, and the fact that most EHDI programs do NOT screen preschoolers' hearing (D).

20. D: In audiology, MCL stands for Most Comfortable Loudness (D). This is the volume at which sound is neither too loud nor too quiet. In audiological examinations, the measure in decibels (dB) assigned to an individual's hearing threshold reflects a loudness at which that person can hear a pure tone *half* of the time. Therefore, we may still be able to hear sounds at a quieter level than we prefer, yet we feel uncomfortable with that level. Conversely, some sounds may not be loud enough to damage our hearing, yet we are still uncomfortable if we find them too loud. Maximum Comfort Level (A) and Minimum Clarity Locutions (B) are invented choices. Medial Cochlear Ligaments (C) is an invented choice as well.

21. C: Aphasia in general refers to the spontaneous loss of language function. Different types of aphasia can affect different components of language usage. Broca's aphasia primarily affects expressive oral or spoken language, though other aspects of language usage can be affected as well. Broca's aphasia primarily stems from damage to the Broca's area of the frontal lobe of the brain. Broca's aphasia often presents with difficulty forming grammatically correct sentences. In many cases, individuals with Broca's aphasia have a latency in speech production and common functional words are omitted in speech production.

22. B: Introducing sound-spellings (A) is for teaching students which written letters correspond to which spoken sounds, which they must know *before* learning to decode words. Discriminating individual phonemes within words (C) is for teaching students phonological awareness, which they also must have *before* decoding new words. Reviewing sound-spellings to overlearn them (D) is for phonics maintenance rather than word decoding. Blending phonemes into words (B) is for helping students learn a strategy to apply their sound-spelling learning to decoding unfamiliar words.

23. B: The normal way a /t/ or /d/ is produced in English is by pressing the tip of the tongue against the alveolar ridge (B). In some American regional dialects, such as in working-class populations in areas of New York, Massachusetts or Connecticut, these sounds may be made with the tongue touching the upper teeth (A), but this is a dialect or what many people call an "accent." When pressing the tongue against the alveolar ridge, no other sounds but /t/ or /d/ are possible. (The only difference between the two is that /t/ is unvoiced while /d/ is voiced.) When the tongue is in close contact with the alveolar ridge but not pressed against it, allowing some air through, the unvoiced or voiced fricatives /s/ or /z/ are produced. Pressing the back of the tongue against the place where the soft palate (C) meets the hard palate (D) produces the sounds /k/ or /g/ in the case of plosives, and by not pressing firmly produces / ʃ/ or /ʒ/ in the case of fricatives. (Affricates combine an alveolar stop with a fricative, such as /tʃ/as in "cha-cha" or /dʒ/ as in "judge.")

24. A: The most likely explanation for this example is (A): Marco's first (native) language is influencing his second language. In Castilian, one dialect of Spanish, the letter "c" when followed by a vowel is not pronounced as /s/ as it is in English and in Catalan, South American, and other dialects of Spanish, but as /θ/ or theta, represented in the English alphabet as "th" (devocalized as in "thin" or "math," not vocalized as in "this" or "that"). With the similarities between Spanish and English, Marco is transferring his Spanish pronunciation to his English pronunciation. If the SLP does not find any physiological or possible neurological deficits in testing Marco, it is likely he is not showing a systematic articulation disorder (B) in which a person regularly mispronounces a certain phoneme or phonemes. Broca's aphasia (C) is a language disorder that is typically secondary to some form of traumatic brain injury. This is a speech issue, not a language issue; and there is nothing in the question to give the impression that Marco has any sort of injury, which makes this answer unlikely. Considering Marco is now able to speak two languages fluently and the passage gives no indication that he has any other articulation or phonological speech errors, an undiagnosed case of CAS (D) is very unlikely.

25. D: Apraxia of speech is caused by neurological damage localized to the brain's left hemisphere. Neurological damage localized to the basal ganglia control circuit (A) does not cause speech apraxia but does cause the hypokinetic and hyperkinetic types of dysarthria, characterized respectively by rigid or involuntary speech movements. Neurological damage localized to the cerebellar control circuit (B) also does not cause apraxia but does cause the ataxic type of dysarthria, characterized by uncoordinated speech movements. Neurological damage localized to the brain's right hemisphere (C) does not cause motor speech disorders (apraxia or dysarthrias) but can cause receptive aphasia (a language disorder) and other symptoms in addition to language problems.

26. A: ASHA reports that federal officials state that the IDEA (Individuals With Disabilities Education Act) takes precedence in determining the confidentiality requirements of student records. The FERPA (B) or Family Educational Rights and Privacy Act protects the privacy of student records maintained by agencies (or their agents) with federal funding but does not supersede the IDEA's confidentiality requirements. The HIPAA (C) or Health Insurance Portability and Accountability Act regulates the confidentiality of medical information via patient privacy rules but does not supersede the confidentiality requirements of the IDEA regarding student records.

27. C: Of the choices offered, this is the only one that an SLP can ethically do. It is permissible to give clients, family members, or prospective clients general informational or educational communications via e-mail, messaging, written letters, or other correspondence. However, it violates Principle of Ethics I of the ASHA Code of Ethics, Rule C, to discriminate in delivering professional services on the basis of religion (D), age, race, ethnicity, gender, gender identity, sexual orientation, national origin, or disability. It violates Rule K of this same principle to provide clinical services only by correspondence {(A), (B)}.

28. D: Presbycusis, or age-related hearing loss, is most often characterized by (D) more hearing loss at higher frequencies. More loss at lower frequencies (A) is not typical of hearing loss associated with aging and is unusual in general. More loss at middle frequencies (B) is also unusual. While early noise-induced hearing loss can cause a sharp drop in acuity around 4,000 Hz, this is not so much a middle frequency as a medium-high frequency. Uniform loss at all frequencies (C) is not characteristic of presbycusis specifically or of sensorineural losses in general, but is more often found with conductive hearing losses. With presbycusis, the higher the frequency, the more loss is seen. This accounts for the difficulty people with age-related hearing loss have with discrimination of words containing high-frequency consonant sounds such as /s/, /t/, /f/, etc.

29. B: The phonemes /k/ and /g/ are stops, produced using the same placement and positioning—with the back of the tongue against the velum in the back of the oral cavity—with the only difference being that the former is devocalized and the latter is vocalized. Because of the tongue placement, these phonemes are called *back* or *backed.* Kenny is using /t/ and /d/, which are the unvoiced and voiced versions of the stop produced by placing the tip of the tongue against the alveolar ridge in the front of the mouth, hence these are called *front* or *fronted.* He is substituting backed phonemes with fronted phonemes, not vice versa (B). Neither the /k/ and /g/ nor the substituted /t/ and /d/ represent middle {(C), (D)} phonemes, which are made with the tongue below (and touching) the hard palate in the middle of the oral cavity, for example, /ʃ/ ("sh"), /ʒ/ ("zh"), /tʃ/ ("ch"), or /dʒ/ ("j").

30. C: Chomsky's theory proposes innate, "hard-wired" biological capacities like a Language Acquisition Device (LAD) and universal generative grammar enable children's language development. This supports the observation that children of all cultures develop language in the same stages and patterns around the same ages. Skinner's behaviorist theory, which emphasizes environmental influences (A), is less compatible: Children acquire language faster than they could through conditioning processes; they could not generate the infinite sentences possible via imitation; they learn without regular adult correction; and they overregularize irregular verbs without adult modeling. Whorf's linguistic relativity hypothesis (B) is also less compatible because Whorf proposed language differentially influences people's thinking by culture (e.g., Eskimo languages have far more words for snow than English). Neural networks (D) propose children learn similarly to computer systems with no preprogramming via exposure to many language examples. As this would vary among cultural contexts, it is also less compatible with universal language development than Chomsky's ideas.

31. D: Computer software with a voice synthesizer produces a digital voice for those who cannot speak. Most of the time, a student who needs this type of assistance will have a device called an augmentative and alternative communication (AAC) device that contains the software and hardware needed to run a voice synthesizer for real-time communications. This differs from text-to-speech software in that AACs contain special programming that allow the user to quickly string together words for real-time communication. Text-to-speech software requires typing and is not accessible enough to function in real communication for most people. Speech-to-text software (A) allows a person to speak into a computer microphone and the program produces typed text of the spoken language. This helps those who can speak but cannot write or type. Text-to-speech software (B) also produces a synthesized voice to read text, but these programs typically scan the text and read it aloud to assist those with visual impairments and reading difficulties, not to supply a substitute speaking voice. Voice recognition software (C) also transcribes spoken language into typed text, similar to the closed-captioning feature on televisions.

32. A: Research has found that in elementary school-age children, working memory (a) increases with age. In the age group of 7 to 13 years, working memory is found to improve significantly as children get older. Working memory in this age group does not (b) decrease with age. It does not (c) stay the same but makes gains. It does not (d) fluctuate over time but grows in capacity with maturation.

33. D: The abducent (D) nerve, CN VI, innervates the lateral eye muscles. The olfactory (A) nerve, CN I, transmits sensory impulses of smell. The optic (B) nerve, CN II, transmits sensory impulses of vision. The auditory (C) nerve, CN VIII, transmits sensory impulses of hearing.

34. D: The SVO word order is used by the most speakers of different world languages (including Albanian, Greek, all Germanic and Romance languages, etc.). The SOV (A) word order is used in the largest number of *languages* (including Turkish, Hungarian, Armenian, Korean, Japanese, Burmese, Basque, Hindi, Bengali, etc.) rather than of speakers. The VSO (B) word order is preferred in Arabic, Hebrew, Irish, Gaelic, Welsh, and others. The VOS (C) word order is used in only a few languages, including Northwest American and Canadian Indian tribal languages. (Note: English, like Russian and Latin, allows varying word orders.)

35. A: The "guess the word" game described teaches the phonological process of blending phonemes, i.e., combining individual speech sounds into whole words. Deleting phonemes (B) would involve having students change words by removing one speech sound from each word to create a new one, e.g., from "brat" to "bat." Segmenting phonemes (C) would involve separating words into their individual component phonemes, e.g., "sun" to "s," "u," and "n." Substituting phonemes (D) would involve changing words by replacing one phoneme in each word with another, e.g., from "sun" to "fun."

36. D: Internal consistency is the measure of reliability that estimates how similar all the items on one test are, that is, how well they correlate with each other. This measure is used often with norm-referenced tests. Test-retest reliability (A) measures how similar the results of a test will be when its administration to the same examinees is repeated after a short time. This shows how much a test can produce consistent scores. Parallel forms reliability (B) measures how similar multiple, parallel forms of a test are to one another. (Many standardized tests are designed with a Form A, Form B, and so on.) This measure estimates how consistent you can expect the same examinees' scores to be across the test forms. Decision consistency reliability (C) is often used with criterion-referenced tests that classify results as pass–fail rather than giving numerical scores or scaled ratings. If the same examinee either passes or fails in two separate administrations, the test yields consistent decisions. (This method can apply to parallel-forms or test-retest administrations.)

37. C: Donald's therapists would find it most effective to practice differential reinforcement of attempts and successive approximations (C). The time and effort required of Donald indicates as much reward and encouragement as possible. However, reinforcing all his attempts (B) could mislead or confuse him regarding the target words, as the goal is not made clear. Similarly, reinforcing both his attempts and successive approximations in the same way (D) does not help him differentiate between all attempts and vocalizations that more closely approach a target word. Giving him one kind of reinforcement for attempts will encourage him to keep trying over the long time period he requires. Giving a different kind of reinforcement for successive approximations toward the target word will give him feedback that he is coming closer to the word, shaping his vocalizations. Only reinforcing his eventual correct utterance of a target word (A) is not realistic when it takes him years to learn one word, as too much time will elapse without any rewards for his efforts toward the end result.

38. B: Profound sensorineural hearing loss means that the hair cells in the Organ of Corti at the cochlea no longer function. This type of hearing loss cannot be remedied by hearing aids, which amplify the sound signal and require that the patient have sufficient residual hearing, which is not the case with profound hearing loss. Cochlear implants, however, are surgically implanted, bypass the outer and middle ears, and perform the function of converting the acoustic energy of sounds into electrical energy when the cochlear hair cells can no longer do this. Therefore, (C) and (D) are incorrect.

39. C: When liquids are aspirated, they go into the lungs instead of the stomach. This often results in lung infection, that is, aspiration pneumonia. Dehydration (A) is more related to the inability to swallow enough water and foods with high water content. If a dysphagia patient cannot swallow enough for sufficient hydration, he or she is given supplemental fluids via feeding tube or injection. Malnutrition (B) is more related to not swallowing enough foods and liquids containing necessary nutrients, requiring supplementation. Asphyxiation (D) or suffocation is related more to aspiration of solids that block the airway, preventing breathing.

40. C: The normal adult human eating and swallowing processes involve more than 30 different muscles and nerves. These processes do not involve more than 40 (A), fewer than 20 (B), or fewer than 10 (D) muscles and nerves.

41. C: Students who score in the below-average range on achievement tests with no other concerns will typically fall under the "specific learning disability" category. Students with specific learning disabilities have deficits in the areas of reading, writing, and math. It is important to understand the results of assessments in order to appropriately place students and provide services that the student will need. Answer A is incorrect because students with trouble in speech or communication would take a test specific to those needs. Answer B is incorrect because students who receive services under the other health impairment category will have a health impairment that impacts their access to education. Answer D is incorrect because a cognitive disability is not one of the disability categories under the Individuals with Disabilities Education Act.

42. C: Those influenced by Piaget's theory of cognitive development (C) have found the role of learning processes to be more important than previously thought. Piaget believed that children learn by interacting with and acting upon their environments, and that in so doing, they construct knowledge (constructivism). These beliefs are compatible with placing more importance on learning processes than on inherent structures (D), such as a language acquisition device (LAD) and a universal grammar, which are emphasized by nativist theories. While most theories recognize the interaction of nature and nurture (A & B) to some degree, those subscribing to Piaget's models have come to feel since the 1980s that learning processes play a more important role than previously realized.

43. B: Educational research into teaching practices for nonverbal communication is notably lacking; however, teachers who have experimented with lessons (cf. Darn, 2014) have discovered it is best to teach nonverbal communication skills in small chunks (A), using appropriate situations (B) wherein the context of the theme or situation is congruent with the language. They also find that to help students use gestures and expressions to reinforce linguistic meaning, teachers must include drama-based instructional activities that build student confidence (C) and creativity (D).

44. C: *Positive predictive value* is defined as the proportion, out of all children screened and identified as at risk for an ASD, who actually fail the follow-up testing. The positive predictive value of a screening tool is inversely correlated with a disorder's base rate, that is, its prevalence. ASDs have comparatively low incidence, so the probability of a positive screening result's indicating the child actually has an ASD is lower. *Sensitivity* (A) is defined as the percentage of true positives, that is, of children identified as at risk by the screening who fail follow-up testing or are diagnosed with

ASD. *Specificity* (B) is defined as the percentage of true negatives, that is, of children with negative screening results who also passed follow-up testing or had ASD ruled out as a diagnosis. *Negative predictive value* (D) is defined as the proportion of all children the screening identified as not at risk who also pass follow-up testing.

45. A: It is not true that nasal emission is a nasal resonance problem (A). Nasal emission is nasal noise caused by air escaping through the nose when there is incomplete velopharyngeal closure. Though it is not a disorder of nasal resonance per se, it often accompanies hypernasality (B) when the etiology is structural. In addition to weakened movement of the velum and pharynx, a short palate can cause nasal emissions, so these can be symptomatic of palatal insufficiency (C). It is true that nasal emission rarely occurs for functional reasons (D). It is nearly always related to some structural inadequacy.

46. B: On a continuum, the simplest level of phonological awareness is represented by being able to recognize and produce rhymes in songs, and show understanding that sentences contain individual words by segmenting them (D). Segmenting words into syllables and blending syllables into words (A) represents a more complex level around the middle of the continuum. A higher level of complexity is segmenting words into onsets and rimes and blending onsets and rimes into words (C). The highest level is phonemic awareness, i.e., understanding that words contain individual phonemes and being able to manipulate (blend, segment, delete, substitute) these (B).

47. A: In order to assess a student for oral expression abilities, a test to measure their expressive language abilities is most appropriate. Students who struggle with oral expression tend to struggle expressing themselves orally due to many factors. This kind of assessment can guide the data collection needed for instruction in the classroom and skills to work on. Answer B is incorrect because receptive language assessments are more appropriate for students who struggle with language input rather than output. Answer C is incorrect because auditory discrimination tests are used for students who struggle with different sounds. Answer D is incorrect because this kind of assessment would be more appropriate in measuring a student's cognitive abilities.

48. C: According to ASHA, the SLP will often need to counsel parents wanting advice about whether to try hearing aids (which benefit some children but not others) or ASL while awaiting cochlear implant surgery, and this is within the SLP's scope of services. Of course, deaf educators as available can counsel parents about ASL (A), but this does not mean the SLP cannot do so in addition to or in lieu of a deaf educator or ASL specialist. Counseling on this issue is not restricted to the surgeon (B). Audiologists fit and test hearing aids and can counsel parents in this case (D) but are not the only ones to help parents decide whether to use them. Families in this situation frequently look to the SLP for advice, which SLPs can give based on their experience with other families and data from published parents' reports.

49. A: Principles of language disorder treatment for the youngest children include early detection and intervention, greater parent involvement, and promoting social interaction through linguistic communication. For younger children, focusing on more functional results is more appropriate; increasing functional flexibility (B) is more appropriate for school-age children. Treatment of school-age children progresses at a slower rate than treatment of younger children, not vice versa (C). Treatment in the least-restrictive environment (D) is mandated by law for students in public schools, not for younger children, for whom the home or naturalistic environments are more appropriate.

50. B: Research has long since established (e.g., studies dating back to 1992–1994) that psychometric review of tests for evaluating preschool language skills can identify such tests that meet half or even more of the psychometric criteria (A); and the review of the tests can attain high inter-rater reliability (D); and yet, these tests can still be inaccurate for differentiating children with normal language skills and those with impaired language skills. Researchers therefore advise evaluators of the need for using BOTH psychometric review AND data-based validation procedures, but NOT substituting data-based validation procedures alone for psychometric review (C).

51. B: When children start school with language deficits, these deficits infringe on their ability to learn, to be empowered personally, to communicate with others both verbally and nonverbally, and on their developing social relationships. It is not true that families cause language deficits by preferring reading about news and current affairs over literature (A). While it is preferable for families to expose their children to reading of both kinds of materials, a family's emphasis on any kind of reading is more beneficial than its lack. While language deficits often cause children to perform below ability on school assessments, such test results do NOT reflect true intelligence deficits (C); rather, assessors may wrongly attribute such substandard performance to lower intelligence when it is really due to lower language skills. It is also NOT true that children's language development is not influenced by how much or how little their peers value reading (D): Peer groups have great influence on children, including the relative importance they accord to reading.

52. B: Like the Shaker exercise, the hyoid lift maneuver (B) does not involve swallowing. In this exercise, a sheet of paper placed on a towel is picked up by sucking on a straw and moved to a container into which it is dropped by the release of suction. The goal is to move several sheets of paper into the container in each session. The Mendelsohn maneuver (A) involves consciously keeping the larynx lifted, while swallowing. This exercise is to be repeated several times a day. The effortful swallow (C) involves swallowing while squeezing the swallowing muscles as hard as possible. Three sets per day are done, with each set consisting of 5-10 attempts. The supraglottic swallow (D) involves holding the breath while swallowing, then coughing (to clear anything that went down past the vocal cords). It is to be done first without food and can be done with food later as proficiency increases.

53. B: The ossicles (meaning "tiny bones") consist of the malleus (or hammer), incus (or anvil), and stapes (or stirrup) and are located in the middle ear. The pinna (A) (meaning "feather"), or auricle, is the visible ear structure on the outside of the head in humans. It collects and funnels sound waves. These waves pass through the ear canal (C) or external auditory meatus. When the sound waves reach the middle ear, the ossicles function to amplify and transmit them to the inner ear (D), where the hair cells in the cochlea convert them from acoustical energy to electrical energy, which is then transmitted via the auditory or acoustic nerve to the brain. Sound sensations are interpreted by the brain's auditory cortex to become sound perceptions.

54. A: The only true statement is that (A) three genes causing stuttering have now been identified and isolated. This was done for the first time by researchers at the National Institute on Deafness and other Communication Disorders (NIDCD) in 2010. Stuttering can occur as a result of acute stroke or TBI and is therefore not specifically genetic in natrure (B). It is not true that developmental stuttering is not found to run in families (C); researchers have found that developmental stuttering is more frequent in members of the same family. It is also not true that stuttering that runs in a family is attributed to environmental factors (D) such as reinforcement. Developmental stuttering running in families is attributed to genetic factors, which is supported by the recent isolation of genes causing some cases of it (A).

55. C: Students with SLI have the best prognosis if their problems are mostly with phonology (C), i.e., speech sounds. They may have trouble recognizing, discriminating among, sequencing, and/or producing speech sounds correctly. Students having problems with syntax (A), i.e., sentence structure (including verb tenses, persons, and other grammatical constructions) and word order; with prosody (B), i.e., the rhythms and intonation patterns of speech; and with semantics (D), i.e., the meanings of words and their uses in context, all have difficulties with linguistic processing, which yield poorer cognitive, educational, and social prognoses compared to those for SLI students with only phonological or articulation difficulties.

56. C: The ataxic type of dysarthria, characterized by incoordination of the speech movements, is caused by neurological damage localized to the cerebellar control circuit. The flaccid (A) type of dysarthria, characterized by weakness of the speech movements, is caused by neurological damage localized to the lower motor neurons. The spastic (B) type of dysarthria, characterized by spasticity or hypertonicity of the speech movements, is caused by neurological damage localized to the upper motor neurons. The hypokinetic (D) type of dysarthria, characterized by rigidity of speech movements and problems with scaling speech movements, is caused by neurological damage localized to the basal ganglia control circuit.

57. C: The Toronto Tests of Receptive Vocabulary (C), or TTRV, assesses knowledge of word meaning with both English and Spanish words. These tests contain an equal number of words (40) in each language. English and Spanish word choices are not identical. The Picture Vocabulary subtest of the TOLD (A), or Test of Language Development, does not include Spanish words. Neither does the Peabody Picture Vocabulary Test (PPVT) (B) or the Assessment of Children's Language Comprehension (ACLC) test (D).

58. C: Research finds that more than 10 percent of all speech problems are caused by varying degrees of hearing loss, including mild losses. Choice (A) represents a proportion much greater than the reality. Choices (B) and (D) represent proportions lower than the fact.

59. C: *Co-articulation* means the phonemes in the words we speak are influenced by nearby phonemes. This makes them both variable and difficult to isolate or segment. Co-articulation is responsible for the evolution of "inpossible" to "impossible": The bilabial articulation of /p/ influenced the consonant /n/ to become the bilabial /m/. Co-articulation prevents phonemes from being linear in production (A). It also keeps spoken phonemes from being invariant, that is, each one having only a single waveform representation (B). While we visually perceive colors on a continuum (e.g., we see red-orange between red and orange, blue-violet between blue and violet, etc.), we do NOT aurally perceive sounds on a continuum (D): We hear a syllable as *either* /pa/ *or* /ba/ but not as something in between because the two have different voice onset times (VOTs). Our separation of such different sounds facilitates our comprehension of speech and is known as *categorical perception.*

60. A: The semantic intervention most similar to Sentence Completion is the cloze format (A). This format can be oral or written. The only difference is that the missing word the child must supply can be in any part of the sentence, while in Sentence Completion the missing word is always at the end of the sentence. Therefore, Sentence Completion is better for learning semantic rules for choosing words, relationships, or concepts that come at the end of a phrase or sentence, while cloze has a wider range of application. Examples of sentence completion using prototypical contexts are "I take my coat ___ (off/on/over); I put my shoes ____ (in/on/over)." Examples of sentence completion using verbal analogies are "Trees have leaves and birds have _______ (feathers); John is my uncle and Mary is my ____ (aunt); you drive a car and you fly a ____ (plane)." Cloze may use a paragraph in which certain parts of speech such as prepositions, as used in the first sentence completion example, are left blank throughout: "Billy has a green rug __ on the floor __ his room. There is a poster of a tiger __ the wall ____ his bed and a desk ___ to the window. He has an aquarium ___ fish _ them." Riddles (B) are good for teaching the consolidation of labels or names of things, animals, or people, i.e., teaching referential vocabulary. 20 Questions (C) is good for teaching verbal specificity by narrowing down groups of words according to their semantic class or to their shared features of meaning. Role playing (D) is good for teaching appropriate word, phrase, or sentence choices according to the social context.

61. D: There is no evidence to suggest a correlation between phonological development delays and muscular development delays (D). However, according to research findings, preschool-aged children with delayed phonological development are likely to also have delayed morphological (A), syntactic (B), and discourse structure development (C). In addition, young children typically demonstrate better phonological performance when uttering individual words and verbal labels for pictures than connected conversational speech and organized, syntactically complex narratives.

62. C: The transverse arytenoid (C) is the only unpaired muscle in the larynx. The intrinsic paired laryngeal muscles are the cricothyroid (A), lateral cricoarytenoid, oblique arytenoids (B), transverse arytenoid, posterior cricoarytenoid, superior thyroarytenoid (D), thyroarytenoid-muscularis, and thyroarytenoid-vocalis.

63. C: Less reaction by the child to the parents' focus on the child (c) is not a characteristic of this family pattern according to Dr. Bowen's theory. In fact, the opposite is true: Bowen states that the more the parents focus overly on a child with some impairment, the more the child reciprocally focuses on the parents, their expectations, their needs, and their attitudes, and reacts more to these than his or her siblings do. Bowen finds that this reactivity of the child can impede his or her school performance, social relationships, and health. Excessive worry about the child by one or both parents (a) is characteristic of this pattern. Having either an overly idealized view of the child (b) or an overly negative view of the child (d) is also symptomatic of this family relationship pattern.

64. D: All types of dysarthrias can include hypernasal speech resonance as a characteristic; in many types, it always occurs, and in some, it is sometimes present. Cleft palate (B) typically always causes hypernasality due to the palatal opening between the mouth and nose. Speech apraxia (C), which causes difficulty with coordinating speech movements, can cause inconsistent nasality but not consistent hypernasality throughout the speech, as (A) and (B) do.

65. A: The palatal lift is a prosthetic device that raises the velum in cases of inadequate velar mobility. It is helpful in cases of velopharyngeal incompetence, which is caused by physiological defects, such as neurological conditions like dysarthria and apraxia, neuromuscular disorders like myasthenia gravis, hypotonia (= weak muscle tone), and other problems with muscle function. The palatal obturator (B) is a prosthetic device used to close an open cleft or fistula of the palate. The speech bulb obturator (C) is a prosthetic device used to close the nasopharynx, which typically applies to velopharyngeal insufficiency (due to an anatomical defect rather than velopharyngeal incompetence due to a physiological defect). Prostheses do not permanently correct these problems as surgery can, but they DO work (D) to improve them in cases where surgery is contraindicated or as temporary measures.

66. A: A functional magnetic resonance imaging scan (fMRI) shows images of the metabolic function of different parts of the brain. In both MRI and fMRI, the magnetic field and gradient coil of the machine use atomic physics principles for brain imaging. However, the MRI (B) scan gives 3-D pictures of the brain's anatomical structure only, whereas the fMRI scan gives pictures of the brain's metabolic function, showing which regions are more or less active during various cognitive processes. EEG (C) or electroencephalography records the brain's electrical rather than metabolic activity, showing normal or abnormal brain waves. A PET (D) or positron emission tomography scan shows relative metabolic brain activity as an fMRI does but by measuring glucose in different brain areas, whereas an fMRI measures alignment in the brain's water molecules, indicating which areas need more oxygen. The need for more glucose and more oxygen both signal greater activity. However, a key difference is that the PET scan is invasive because it requires injecting radioactive glucose into the patient, while the fMRI is noninvasive.

67. C: Clara's words will all very likely be in the correct order and meaningful within the context of her own sentence; (C) however, their meaning within the context of a conversation will be tenuous or nonexistent. People with Wernicke's aphasia often speak fluently and with correct syntax. However, while they can express themselves in speech, their ability to process and understand the speech of others is significantly impaired (A). Therefore, though Clara's speech makes sense, eventually its meaning will break down due to the lack of feedback (B) from other people's speech which she cannot understand. Clara is likely to develop strategies, as most Wernicke's aphasia patients do, to compensate for and hide her lack of comprehension (D). For example, if asked "Where did you go yesterday?" and she cannot understand what you said, she may respond with something like, "Oh my, what a pretty dress you have on!" in an attempt to hide the fact that she doesn't know what you asked her, and to divert attention in the hope of having a successful social interaction. Clara's disorder is thought to be caused by damage to Wernicke's area, in the posterior of the superior temporal gyrus in the cerebral cortex, around the auditory cortex, on the Sylvian fissure where the temporal and parietal lobes of the brain meet. New research suggests that functions traditionally attributed to Wernicke's area take place more widely in the temporal and frontal lobes as well.

68. B: Principle of Ethics IV, Rule B of the ASHA Code of Ethics states that SLPs "shall prohibit anyone under their supervision from engaging in any practice that violates the Code of Ethics." Therefore, this is NOT the responsibility of the supervisee (A) but of the supervisor. Principle of Ethics I, Rule F states that SLPs with ASHA's CCC may delegate clinical, service-provision-related tasks to others "only if those services are appropriately supervised, realizing that the responsibility for client welfare remains with the certified individual." Therefore, the supervisor and NOT the delegated staff are responsible for client welfare (C). Principle of Ethics I, Rule E states that SLPs with the CCC will NOT delegate tasks requiring professional "skills, knowledge, and judgment" to any nonprofessionals they supervise (D).

69. B: Focusing on pragmatics, that is, how the stutterer uses speech and language in everyday interactions, is included among indirect treatment approaches. Modeling a slower speech rate (A), practicing relaxed breathing techniques (C), and allowing the stutterer to finish a statement without interrupting (D) are all methods of direct approaches to stuttering therapy.

70. A: Improvement of less than 20 percent after 3 months is equally likely to be due to chance as to treatment. This does not indicate slow but adequate improvement (B). Inaccurate measurement is a possibility but is only one variable and not necessarily the reason for this number (C). While lack of progress beyond chance suggests that the therapy chosen is ineffective, this does not automatically mean the program should be discarded and replaced (D) with an entirely different therapy program. There are often relatively minor adjustments or changes to a therapy program that can make a great difference in its efficacy. These should be investigated and tried before scrapping the entire program for another.

71. A: One characteristic of individuals with cognitive communication disorders is that their speech remains fluent, and they retain the ability to use the meanings and structures of language correctly. This often makes language assessment batteries designed with aphasia patients in mind unsuitable for cognitive communication-disordered patients, as these tests do not evaluate conversation and thus will not reveal the true extent of the problem, which includes impairment in the ability to organize their thoughts, respond to what others say focusing on the main point or topic, and take turns in conversations (B). Cognitive communication disorders also involve difficulties with understanding and using the pragmatics of language (C), like "reading" social contexts accurately and responding appropriately, and impairment in executive functions (D), like decision making, planning, goal setting, problem solving, flexibility, self-control, self-monitoring, and self-evaluation.

72. D: Volume (D) is not a variable that is assessed in stuttering disorders. Rate (A) refers to the speed at which one speaks. Many stutterers speak too fast. Others slow or stop their speech in their struggle to get the words out. Slowing down can often help stutterers in combination with other strategies. However, when some stutterers struggle too hard to get a word out without repetition or prolongation, the tension can cause blocking, i.e., their speech is completely stopped, which is counterproductive. Many stutterers also show disordered speech rhythms (B), alternately speeding up and slowing down, prolonging vowel or consonant sounds, or having parts—words, phrases, or sentences—within their overall speech flow that are faster or slower than what sounds normal. Fluency (C) refers to the speaker's ability to speak easily without undue effort and with normal rate and rhythm. There is a class of stutterers known as "fluent stutterers" who do stutter but without interrupting, slowing, or stopping their speech. These are usually mild stutterers.

73. B: Echolalia is (B) repeating what other people say. People who display this behavior may only repeat what others say exclusively and never make any original utterances of their own, or they may be able to both engage in purposeful speech and in repetition at times. Echolalia is not repeating oneself (A). It is not hearing echoes of speech (C). Difficulty with voice modulation (D), the ability to control the volume of one's speech, can be a symptom of various voice disorders; however, echolalia specifically refers to the repetition of other people when they speak.

74. B: The oldest of the choices is the cerebral dominance theory (A), an organic theory developed in the 1930s by Orton and Travis and proposing that stuttering resulted from lack of coordination between the brain's hemispheres when one side was not dominant. The diagnostic theory (D), a behavioral theory, was developed by Wendell Johnson in the 1940s and 1950s and proposed that stuttering was differentially conditioned by different parental responses to young children's normal dysfluencies. The psychological theory (C) that stuttering was a neurotic symptom best treated by psychotherapy has since been disproven by research findings that psychotherapy was not effective for stuttering; hence, it is not the most recent. The covert repair hypothesis is the most recent of the choices, proposing that stutterers have poor phonological encoding skills, leading to flawed phonetic plans, and that their dysfluencies are normal repair responses to these abnormal phonetic plans.

75. A: On the ALS Severity Scale, at the mildest level, a patient swallows normally, progressing to some abnormalities; to minor difficulties with swallowing; to taking smaller bites and longer times to chew and swallow; to requiring a diet of only soft foods; to requiring a diet of only liquids; to needing a liquid diet supplemented with tube feedings (C); to requiring mostly tube feeding with only occasional liquefied foods by mouth; to not being able to take any nourishment by mouth (D); to needing medications to reduce mucosal, salivary, and other secretions or having secretions suctioned out (B) due to inability to swallow them; to ultimately aspirating these secretions, that is, inhaling them through the airways into the lungs instead of swallowing them through the esophagus into the stomach. Aspiration is very dangerous: It can cause pneumonia or death.

76. A: Consonant digraphs combine two consonants to make a single sound, e.g., *ch*, *sh*, *th*, *wh*, *ck*, and ng. The word "shocking" contains three consonant digraphs: *sh-*, *-ck-*, and *-ng*. Consonant blends combine two or three consecutive consonant sounds, e.g., *bl*, *cl*, sc, *sm*, *scr*, *spl*, *spr*, *str*, etc.

"Screams" (B) contains the *scr* consonant blend. "Splashes" (C) contains the *spl* consonant blend, plus the consonant digraph *sh*. "Smoking" (D) contains the consonant blend *sm*, plus the consonant digraph *-ng*.

77. A: The unobstructed (= no blockage) form of nasal air emission during speech affects the air pressure inside the oral cavity. The obstructed (= blockage) form has NO effect on intra-oral breath pressure {(B), (C)}. Air escaping through the nostrils occurs during the production of consonant sounds, not vowels (D) because it occurs during the production of sounds involving air pressure, which vowel sounds do not.

78. D: Research finds that ADHD (Attention Deficit Hyperactivity Disorder) often coexists with communication disorders. Researchers also find that many individuals with ADHD have neurological deficits in executive function, or higher-order cognitive skills. Phonological disorders represent deficits in processing patterns and systems in speech and language, which is a higher-order cognitive function. School phobia (A) is a social phobia involving abnormal fear of school. Depression (B) involves feelings of excessive sadness or hopelessness, social withdrawal, apathy, and so on. Anxiety (C) involves excessive worrying and fears. While any of these could and might coexist with a phonological disorder, none of them is found to coexist with phonological disorders any more often than other conditions, unlike ADHD, which is.

79. A: A baby's cries differentiate (B) to indicate different needs such as hunger, pain, etc., between birth and 3 months of age. At this age they also smile when they see their parents and make cooing and gooing sounds (C). Babies engage in vocal play and babbling (A) between 4 and 6 months of age. At this age they also use vocalizations and gestures to communicate needs and wants to parents. Babies typically start to utter their first words around the ages between 7 and 12 months.

80. B: An audiogram with a sharp "notch" or "bite" showing a drop in acuity around 4,000 Hz, with the other frequencies above and below 4,000 showing a higher, flat line, indicates noise-induced hearing loss (B) in its early stages. Exposure to loud noise destroys nerve fibers that receive the 4,000-Hz frequency. A normal hearing curve (A) would show a relatively flat line across all frequencies, with the dB level close to 0, within a range from -10 dB to 25 dB, the standard for normal hearing. Conductive hearing losses (C) tend to show an audiogram curve that is relatively flat, similar to a normal hearing curve except that the dB level is not within normal range (for example, it could be 50 or 80 dB instead of 0 dB). Age-related hearing losses (D) or presbycusis are the most common form of hearing loss. Their audiograms are often described as "ski-slope loss" for their resemblance to a downhill curve, with hearing being best at the low frequencies and dropping at higher frequencies. The downward curve from left to right may be gradual with smaller decreases in acuity from one frequency to the next (higher) frequency; or it may be very steep in cases of the most extreme loss at the highest frequencies; or it may be anything in between.

81. C: Poliomyelitis (commonly known as polio) is a viral disease that affects the nerves and can cause paresis and paralysis. Hence, it is classified as a neurological disorder. Thyromegaly (A) is abnormal enlargement of the thyroid gland, which is classified as a structural lesion. Polymyositis (B) is classified as a disease of the connective tissue. A neoplasm (D) is any abnormal growth, whether benign or malignant. Neoplasms, like thyromegaly, are classified as structural lesions.

82. C: The cognitive approach to language remediation focuses on concepts and socialization rather than directly on language. It has been found to be especially effective with children who have been socially disadvantaged. Self-talk (A) can give more practice to children with learning disabilities; modeling (B) provides examples for children with limited awareness or understanding of their own errors to imitate; and behavioral (D) methods provide structure to children who have difficulty organizing their thoughts or need more systematic than targeted changes.

83. C: A tympanogram evaluates the eardrum and conduction bones by subjecting it to variations of air pressure in the ear canal to test the condition of the tympanic membrane located within the middle ear (C). Otoacoustic emission (OAE) tests are employed when determining inner ear functioning (B), and inspection and palpation of the outer ear (A) are components of a full ear exam. An auditory brainstem response (ABR) test is used in conjunction with OAE tests to determine any infirmities of the auditory nerve (D).

84. B: Spasmodic dysphonia (B) is a voice disorder caused by involuntary muscular movements in the larynx. Because this disorder is physiological in nature, rather than psychological, it is not considered a psychogenic voice disorder. Conversion muteness (A), conversion aphonia (C), and mutational falsetto (D) are all psychogenic in origin, meaning they are not specific to any underlying organic cause.

85. B: Strokes or cerebrovascular accidents (CVAs) are the most frequent causes of aphasia in adults. Alzheimer's, atherosclerotic, and other forms of dementia (A), various illnesses (C), traumatic brain injuries or TBIs (D), and progressive neurological disorders also can cause aphasia, but none of these does so as frequently as strokes do.

86. D: According to experts, teachers can model appropriate listening and speaking behaviors for students when they facilitate book discussions and during everyday conversations with them (A), when giving instruction to both whole classes and small groups (B), in one-to-one conversations they have with students and during classroom media discussions (C), and by thinking aloud specifically about the content they are teaching (D).

87. A: According to the ASHA Code of Ethics, Principle of Ethics III, Rule C, SLPs will only refer clients they have served based on the interest of the client and not based on "any personal interest (C), financial (B) or otherwise." Principle of Ethics IV, Rule J, states that SLPs will not render professional services "without exercising independent professional judgment, regardless of referral source or prescription" (D).

88. A: The type or pattern of error most damaging to reading proficiency is substituting words with similar appearances or spelling but completely different meanings, because this shows a lack of reading for meaning. Substituting synonyms (B) shows some comprehension of word meaning. Substituting like parts of speech (C) shows some comprehension of grammar and syntax. Substituting correct words or closer approximations for errors based on information from the sentence context (D) shows skills in both reading for meaning and self-correction.

89. B: In the stage of complex utterances (c. 48–60 months), children regularly produce utterances longer than six words. However, even though the examples given are each three words long, this does NOT mean they belong in the three-word stage (A) because they also include the use of contractions (can't and it's); the use of future concepts (tomorrow); and the use of more difficult preposition concepts (behind)—all of which develop in the complex utterances stage and are not even typical in the four-word stage (C). Therefore (D) is incorrect.

90. B: In some cases, an endoscope can be inserted for imaging and then also used to remove certain obstructions like polyps or foreign objects. When the obstruction cannot be removed endoscopically, it may be removed surgically. Dilation (A) can be done via inserting an endoscope and using its imaging as a guide, inserting and inflating a balloon, or inserting a bougie that gently expands narrowed parts of the esophagus. Dilation is also used to treat obstructive dysphagia.

However, medication (A) is prescribed for esophageal infections (antibiotics) or esophagitis, heartburn, or GERD (antacids, acid reducers), not to remove obstructions. Exercises {(C), (D)} are prescribed to train the muscles in dysphagia with neurological, muscular, or neuromuscular origins (i.e., problems in the brain, nervous system, or muscles); they do not remove obstructions. Dietary changes (D) can make swallowing easier for dysphagia patients but will not remove obstructions.

91. A: Apraxia of speech is a motor speech disorder caused by neurological damage localized to the brain's left hemisphere, where the motor movements for speech are controlled. Ataxia (B) is a lack of coordination; the ataxic type of dysarthria causes this symptom. Dysarthrias disrupt the brain's muscular control of speech movements, whereas apraxia disrupts the brain's motor programming of speech movements. Anoxia (C) means an absence of oxygen, which if more than momentary, causes brain damage. Hypoxia (D) means a lack of oxygen, which also causes brain damage when of sufficient severity or duration.

92. B: The best strategy is to (b) arrange for an interpreter to attend the meeting with them. This could be a relative or family friend who speaks both languages. If such an individual cannot be identified, community resources can be investigated. Anya should not be asked to relay the information to her parents (a). This is unfair to the student, since she may not be able to remember or explain all the information. Because she is a student, not a professional educator, she should not be expected to be able to explain it. Sending the parents a written report, even translated into their language (c), is inadequate, since it denies them the opportunity for having a face-to-face meeting with all involved personnel, asking questions, providing valuable input, and discussing issues and options. Excusing the parents from meeting and just requesting their signature(s) on the IEP (d) excludes them from the IEP process, in which parents and family, as well as students, should be encouraged to participate.

93. C: Difficulties with decoding words (A) involve problems separating written or printed words into the phonemes their letters represent and hearing and differentiating them. Many experts regard decoding difficulty as the source of most reading problems. Comprehension difficulties (B) result from decoding difficulties (A). Retention difficulties (C) result from difficulties with both comprehension (B) and decoding (A). Thus choice D is incorrect.

94. D: All of these have been reported by families (d). While some families do report experiencing more stress in the family (a) as a result of having a child with a disability, they also report that having a child with a disability can improve their family dynamics (b) out of the additional effort and family interaction the disability demands. Families also find they respond to a disability by focusing more on the child's positive attributes (c), rather than taking them for granted as they might with a normally achieving child.

95. A: The law requires that an IEP (Individualized Education Plan) be written, implemented, and updated regularly for preschoolers and school-age children. To treat language disorders in infants and toddlers {(B), (C)}, the law requires that an IFSP, or Individualized Family Service Plan, be written, implemented, and updated regularly. The IEP applies not only to school-age children (D) but to preschoolers as well.

96. B: Vocal cord nodules are most often caused by vocal abuse or misuse, for example, habitually screaming; talking or singing for prolonged periods of time; excessive muscular tension; allergy symptoms; smoking; drinking caffeine or alcohol, which dry out the vocal cords and throat; or otherwise straining the vocal cords. Nodules are typically bilateral. Vocal cord polyps (A) are sometimes caused by vocal abuse or misuse but not as often as nodules. Polyps are also caused by gastroesophageal reflux disease (GERD) or acid reflux; hypothyroidism; long-term tobacco smoking; or one-time vocal cord trauma like screaming or yelling at a sports event or concert. Therefore, (C) and (D) are also incorrect.

97. B: Ataxic cerebral palsy (B) is distinguished by problems with balance and coordination, unsteady gait, and impaired fine motor control. These are typically accompanied by low muscle tone and tremors. Diplegic cerebral palsy (A) is a type of spastic cerebral palsy usually marked by rigidity or stiffness in the legs, with the arms mildly affected or unaffected. They will typically have trouble walking and their legs will "scissor" together. Dyskinetic cerebral palsy (C) is characterized by uncontrollable movement of the hands, arms, feet, or legs. This will typically present as slow or writhing movements, but can also be rapid or jerky. Their muscle tone can vary from day to day or multiple times a day. Spastic cerebral palsy (D) is associated with increased muscle tone and rigidity that makes movement awkward or difficult. Depending on which parts of the body are affected, further classification is given e.g., diplegic, hemiplegic, and quadriplegic.

98. D: In the Early Production Stage, ELLs begin to use words that they learned in the Pre-production Stage. One word and yes/no responses are common. Conversation is initiated with gesture or one or two words. Children in this stage will verbally respond to an increasingly wider variety of linguistic stimuli.

99. A: Approximately 60 percent of children referred to SLPs for help with their speech have speech sound disorders attributed to genetically based linguistic processing deficits. Hence, they are not in the minority of those referred (B). Those with genetic speech motor control deficits comprise only about 10 percent of those referred, so those with genetic language-processing deficits are a much larger group, not much smaller (C). Those with conductive hearing losses comprise a group roughly half the size of the group with genetically based language-processing deficits (about 30 percent), so (D) is also incorrect.

100. D: When some families move within the same state, IEP forms can vary among school districts. Computer technology helps school SLPs use IEP forms that are the same across the state. This decreases the time needed to become familiar with different IEPs. Computers are a big help, not a distraction (A) at IEP meetings: SLPs can make changes to the initial IEP draft; use a projection screen for all attendees to see the text and changes they are making; and have a printer in the meeting room to print out the final draft for all to sign. Another way computers save time is on correspondence: Experts recommend using e-mail to correspond with parents, teachers, administrators (B), and others. Although each student's needs are individualized, it still helps SLPs to avoid "reinventing the wheel" by computerizing a master list of goals (C) for reference in writing IEPs. The technology makes it easier for SLPs to adjust or tailor IEPs as needed than to write goals from scratch for every plan.

101. D: The symbol /ʃ/ represents the first sound in (D) "She," the "sh" sound. The "s" sound in "sass" (A) is /s/ in the International Phonetic Alphabet. The "f" sound in "fist" (B) is given the symbol /f/. The sound in "cha" (C) as in "cha-cha" is actually a combination of a /t/ sound and the /ʃ/ sound in "she" (D). As such it is represented by the symbol /tʃ/.

102. C: How natural the individual's speech does or does not sound can be quite obvious, both to the SLP and to untrained listeners, and can be rated on a point scale; however, ultimately, this judgment is the most subjective of the choices. The frequency (A) and duration (B) of stuttering and the rate of speech (D) can all be objectively measured because these all involve counting—that is, the number of dysfluencies, the number of seconds in the length of dysfluencies, and the number of syllables or words in a speech sample.

103. B: More than half of the cases of congenital deafness in the United States are genetic rather than environmental (A) in origin. Of these cases of genetic deafness, the majority (70–80 percent) are nonsyndromic. Therefore, fewer cases of genetic deafness are secondary to genetic syndromes (C). While syndromic deafness is always genetic because it is caused by some specific genetic syndrome, nonsyndromic deafness is NOT always genetic in origin (D). It can be caused by genetic mutations or by environmental damage to structures in the hearing mechanism.

104. C: Establishing new pitch (C) is used for hypernasality but not denasality. Some people with hypernasal voices speak with overly high pitches, which increases nasality. Speaking at a lower pitch can contribute to greater oral resonance instead of greater nasal resonance. People with denasalized voices sound congested all of the time. The other four therapy approaches listed can be used with both hypernasality and denasality. Ear training (A) focuses on increasing the patient's ability to hear the differences between oral resonances and nasal resonances, so it can be used for either decreasing or increasing nasality. The target voice models approach (B) consists of recording the patient's voice whenever it has a good balance of oral and nasal resonance, and playing this back for the patient to hear. The patient's own phonation, when its resonance is closest to ideal, becomes the patient's own model and can be used equally for hypernasality and denasality. The explanation of problem approach (D) involves explaining to the patient before beginning any therapy exactly what the patient's speech problem is—overly nasal or not nasal enough (the latter especially with nasal consonants)—and is used with either type of problem.

105. B: Telling the parents what she suspects and recommending treatment without a formal diagnosis would be inappropriate. This speech language pathologist (SLP) is very observant and has a talent for diagnosis as well as being well-educated about and experienced with autism. And SLPs do work with some autistic individuals. Regardless of these things, she is not qualified to make such a diagnosis. This should be done by a licensed psychologist, behavior specialist, or psychiatrist. Telling the parents what she suspects could alarm them unnecessarily—especially if she turns out to be wrong or if a psychological practitioner disagrees and/or makes a different diagnosis. Therefore, option A is incorrect.

Referring the parents to a clinic for more thorough evaluation by qualified psychological personnel is the right thing to do. If her suspicions are confirmed, the diagnosis will be made by someone with credentials to back it up and who can recommend appropriate interventions. Referring to a free clinic is also helpful since the parents cannot afford to pay a private practitioner. Therefore, option B is correct.

Asking the referring kindergarten teacher to tell the parents is as inappropriate as telling them herself, since the teacher is also not qualified to make such a diagnosis. The SLP would also be evading personal responsibility by diagnosing outside of her role but using the teacher to deliver the information, which is not confirmed. Both actions would be unethical. Therefore, option C is incorrect.

Ruling out other physical or medical conditions is a good idea, and an astute physician may recognize early signs of autism just as the SLP did. But this step in itself is insufficient. To recommend a physical checkup and also refer the parents to a clinic for behavioral evaluation would be an acceptable action plan. Therefore, option D is incorrect.

106. A: Some children with autism spectrum disorders (ASDs), intellectual disabilities (ID), and other developmental disabilities are unable to complete standardized tests. Diagnostic interventions or dynamic assessments can be used instead to assess their performance levels. These are NOT very similar to standardized, norm-referenced tests (B). They do not compare scores to sample populations' scores. They are not given uniformly to all children but are individualized. They ARE likely to use observations of the child's spontaneous communication (C) as an authentic assessment method. Due to their specialization, these kinds of assessments are likely to take MORE time to administer than standardized instruments (D).

107. C: Traits that have genes located on different chromosomes are independently assorted traits. The principle of independent assortment says that pairs of alleles for different traits are inherited independently of one another. When one allele from each parent's pair is inherited (A), this reflects the genetic principle of segregation, which states that each parent's pair of alleles separate, so the offspring inherits one allele from each parent. This segregation takes place during the process of meiosis, wherein sex cells are formed (B). According to the principle of independent assortment, inheriting one particular trait does NOT influence whether another different trait is also inherited (D) because different pairs of alleles are inherited independently.

108. B: The feature of mixed nasality in speech is characterized by hypernasality or nasal air emission when producing oral consonants and hyponasality when producing nasal consonants. Consistent hypernasality or consistent hyponasality are especially noticeable in vowel sounds (and can also affect consonants), but mixed nasality is a characteristic of hypernasality and hyponasality, both specifically in consonant production: Oral consonants sound overly nasal, while nasal consonants sound insufficiently nasal.

109. A: Dysarthria is a neurologically caused articulation disorder (A). Damage to the parts of the central nervous system controlling the muscles used for speech is the origin of dysarthria. A learning disability affecting reading (B) is dyslexia. A neurologically caused swallowing disorder (C) is dysphagia. An articulation disorder due to dysfunction of the speech organs (D) rather than of the brain is called dyslalia.

110. A: *Iatrogenic etiology* means the condition (in this case, dysphagia) was caused by physician or medical staff activity, including examination, testing, treatment, manner, diagnosis, and so on. Surgical resection (B) of any of the areas involved in swallowing can cause dysphagia. Dysphagia can be caused by fibrosis (scar tissue) forming as a result of radiation (C) therapy. Dysphagia can also be a side effect of some medications (D). However, introducing caustic materials (A) to the alimentary tract is not a normal medical practice, as these are known to cause tissue damage. The ingestion of caustic matter is more likely to be done accidentally or deliberately by the patient. This etiology is classified under structural lesions as caustic materials will damage the swallowing structures.

111. B: Patients with damage to the right hemisphere of the brain are more likely to experience problems in addition to those with speech and language than are patients with damage to the left (A) hemisphere. Therefore, (C) and (D) are incorrect.

112. B: Hunter syndrome is a metabolic disorder wherein the enzyme iduronate sulfatase is lacking. This enzyme breaks down mucopolysaccharides (long chains of sugar molecules); without it, they build up and cause tissue damage. Among other symptoms, it causes progressive intellectual disability and progressive hearing loss, affecting speech and language. Turner syndrome (A), DiGeorge syndrome (C), and Klinefelter syndrome (D) are all chromosomal syndromes—not metabolic disorders—that can affect speech-language development.

113. A: Phonological disorders are language disorders that affect the phonemic level, entailing cognitive (thinking or/brain) functions that organize speech sounds into contrasting patterns, so they can be differentiated to understand and produce understandable speech. Individuals with phonological disorders are unable to correctly form the sounds of words.

114. C: Divergent thinking (C) is not a tendency or characteristic that would cause difficulty with semantics. Being able to generate a greater variety of alternatives would facilitate ease with semantics. Concrete thinking (A) would contribute to difficulty with semantics as the ability to think abstractly is important to interpreting meanings. Limited imagery (B) would interfere, as would limitations in the ability to use symbols and to conceptualize, since these all require some degree of abstraction and imagination. Narrow perception (D) would interfere with semantic ability in that sticking to only one referent for words or concepts, retaining narrow meanings for words, and not shifting from one semantic-grammatical category to another would all prevent someone from identifying multiple and alternative meanings. Another thing that would interfere with semantics is a limited ability to accomplish simultaneously the logical operations, analyses, and syntheses needed for interpreting spatial, temporal, and other relationships among words, phrases, and clauses.

115. A: This description exemplifies delayed language development. Tommy is 9 years old and has the vocabulary (c. 1,000 words) of a normally developing 3- to 4-year-old. By 5 to 6 years, children normally have vocabularies of around 2,000 words, can count up to 10 things, and can speak in simple, compound, complex, and all other sentence types, while Tommy has not attained any of these by age 9. This does not represent normal development (B). However, delayed language development does not automatically indicate a language disorder (C), which can also include receptive difficulties with understanding others or expressive difficulties with communicating one's thoughts. Intellectual disability (D) is not the only cause for language delays. Additional causes include hearing loss, learning disabilities, premature birth, auditory processing disorders, apraxia, autism, and so on.

116. D: Formative assessments are given throughout the unit for teachers to keep track of what concepts and ideas need to be retaught to students. Unit tests and projects are often thought of as summative rather than formative assessments. Informing teaching with assessments is one of the most important components of formative assessments. English language and literacy development can be tracked through things like testing knowledge of vocabulary and academic language use. Sentence frames can also be used within the assessments.

117. B: While correlation between two independent variables does not constitute causation, the data given here do confirm cause and effect between stuttering and the intervention investigated by all studies in the meta-analysis. This is because (1) in all studies within the meta-analysis, participants were assigned to groups randomly; and (2) the effect size observed by the meta-analysis was statistically significant* because the lower limit of the effect size was above 0.0 (0.0 = no effect). *Therefore, (A) is incorrect. According to the numbers given, the average effect of the intervention was moderate at worst, NOT none, and very effective at best, NOT moderate (C). The average effect found by the meta-analysis of all studies does NOT equal the effect for any individual study (D) or for all of the studies included.

118. A: Differentiating among printed characters is visual discrimination, and getting things in the right order is sequencing. These are both functions that can be impaired in (a) a perceptual disorder. Reasoning disorders (b) would not have these characteristics, but would involve difficulties with making decisions, solving problems, forming concepts, making comparisons, doing calculations, and metacognitive processes. Memory disorders (c) involve difficulties with storage, retrieval, recall, recognition, organization, classification, and interpretation of information. Because (a) is correct, answer (d), none of these, is incorrect.

119. D: All of the diseases named are progressive or degenerative, that is, they cause degeneration or deterioration that progresses or advances over time. In all of these diseases, the patient always experiences problems with motor control, and in each, it is either possible or likely that the patient will also develop dementia.

120. B: One feature of African-American Vernacular English, a dialect, is to substitute /d/ for /ð/ as described. Hence, this is NOT any kind of speech or language disorder at all but rather a phonological feature of this dialect. (Note: if there were a disorder, it would also not be developmental (A) because the parents also demonstrate it, unless the parents had been doing so since childhood.)

121. B: The law requires that treatment for infants and toddlers diagnosed with language disorders include an Individualized Family Service Plan (IFSP) that identifies the specific features of the disorder, the goals of treatment, the strategies and settings to be used, and so on. For school-age children {(A), (D)} and preschoolers {(C), (D)}, the law requires that treatment include an IEP or Individualized Education Plan. These documents are similar, and both should involve the parents and family, but the IFSP reflects the fact that the families of infants and toddlers receive a different level of service because these children are not in school yet and so cannot receive services as part of the school day.

122. B: The original three-stage model of normal eating and swallowing consisted of the oral, pharyngeal, and esophageal stages. The four-stage model consisted of dividing the oral stage into the oral preparatory stage, before the actual swallow, and the oral propulsive stage, wherein the tongue squeezes liquid against and along the palate and backward into the pharynx to begin the pharyngeal stage. The pharyngeal (A) and esophageal (C) stages were not divided into additional stages. There is no such thing as an epigastric stage (D).

123. C: Language registers are different tones, vocabulary, sentence structures, and even volume used in different situations. Consider how speaking during a presentation differs from working in small groups in a classroom. The classroom presentation register often includes things like a strong voice that can be heard by the entire class and a varied tone that keeps the audience's interest. Although being able to pronounce words is important, that has to do with phonology rather than discourse.

124. D: Modifying the teacher's speech to support English learners includes actions such as modifying phonics, syntax, semantics, pragmatics, and discourse. This might mean repeating key words and simplifying the sentence structure. Teachers can also modify their language by incorporating the primary language to support understanding; however, research shows that decreased teacher talking time allows for the student to have more talking time.

125. A: Wernicke's aphasia affects receptive language. The patient described still has fluent expressive speech, but she does not understand what others say. The lack of comprehension of input and feedback from others can make her spoken language somewhat irrelevant. She still understands gestural nonverbal communication. If she had Broca's aphasia (B), her expressive language would be damaged, and she would not speak so fluently, having trouble finding words and arranging them grammatically into sentences. If she had global aphasia (C), she would have damage to both Wernicke's and Broca's areas of the brain and have difficulty with both receptive and expressive language. Despite her fluent speech and expressive language, she is not free of any aphasia (D) because she lacks receptive comprehension. Signs of this are her using "stock" social compliments and questions and not directly answering others' questions.

126. A: Cul-de-sac resonance, appropriately named like a street closed at one end or a blind diverticulum or pouch in the body, results when vocal sound can resonate in the nasal cavity or pharynx but cannot be released because of some obstruction. A hypernasal (B) voice is characterized by too much speech sound resonating in the nose due to factors like cleft palate or a large velopharyngeal opening, while a hyponasal (C) voice is characterized by too little nasal resonance, usually due to upper airway blockage. The correct term for a complete absence of any nasal resonance (D) is *denasality*.

127. A: Researchers identify norm-referenced tests, including norm-referenced reading tests, as better for assessing abstract cognitive levels and criterion-referenced tests as better for assessing concrete cognitive levels. They also identify norm-referenced tests as better for assessing heterogeneous groups and criterion-referenced as better for homogeneous groups (B). Also, norm-referenced tests are better for assessing wider ranges of ability and criterion-referenced for narrower ability ranges (C). Finally, they identify norm-referenced tests as better for assessing wider ranges of outcomes and objectives and criterion-referenced for narrower ranges of these (D).

128. A: Referring the mother to a free reading teacher is a way to improve her reading skills and increase her confidence so that she can participate in her daughter's education. Having a few practice sessions in which Janet's mother gets to participate with both teachers as well as her daughter will further boost her confidence at the beginning and give her ideas about how to work with Janet at home. Therefore option A is correct.

For Mrs. Stroud to work with the mother herself is unrealistic given the constraints on a teacher's time. If Mrs. Stroud knows of free adult education, this would be more practical. Therefore option B is incorrect.

There are two disadvantages in Mrs. Stroud scheduling more time to work with Janet. First, Mrs. Stroud's schedule may make this impossible. Second, it does not involve Janet's mother as an active participant in her daughter's education. Even if this plan were possible, if Mrs. Stroud took on extra work it would result in a missed opportunity to involve Janet's mother. It would also preclude the opportunity to improve an adult's education. Therefore option C is incorrect.

Arranging home tutoring for Janet has several disadvantages. First, tutors normally charge fees. If Mrs. Stroud knows of a free tutoring program, there is no reason to cause Janet's mother the financial burden that would come from hiring a private tutor. Second, the tutor would be filling a role that, given some help, Janet's mother could assume. Third, tutoring would not promote the mother's active participation in Janet's education. Fourth, not helping Janet's mother improve her reading skills misses an opportunity to improve an adult's education, which benefits both mother and daughter. Therefore option D is incorrect.

129. C: The Vagus (X) nerve controls six muscles involved in the swallowing process: the levator veli palatine, palatopharyngeus, salpingopharyngeus, intrinsic laryngeal, cricopharyngeus, and pharyngeal constrictor muscles. The Hypoglossal (XII) nerve also controls six swallowing muscles: the intrinsic tongue muscles and the hyoglossus, geniohyoid, genioglossus, styloglossus, and thyrohyoid muscles. The Trigeminal (V) nerve controls four swallowing muscles: the masticatory, mylohyoid, tensor veli palatini muscles, and the anterior belly of the digastric muscles, while the Facial (VII) nerve controls three: the facial and stylohyoid muscles and the posterior belly of the digastric muscles {(A), (D)}. The Glossopharyngeal (IX) nerve controls one muscle: the stylopharyngeus {(B), (D)}.

130. B: A phoneme (A) is an individual speech sound. A grapheme (C) is an individual written symbol, like an alphabet letter or punctuation mark. A sememe (D) is the meaning carried by a morpheme; e.g., the *-s* at the end of a noun is a morpheme; its sememe is pluralization. A morpheme (B) is the smallest individual meaningful grammatical unit that cannot be broken down further; *-tion* is thus a single morpheme, though it contains multiple phonemes and graphemes. Its sememe might be called verb nominalization.

131. C: Researchers have found that the majority (e.g., 80 percent) of SLPs do feel their roles include counseling their clients, yet the same proportion of SLPs reported their degree programs not having offered any counseling courses. Research has not shown that most SLPs received counseling courses as part of their degree programs {(A), (D)} or that most SLPs feel it is not within their roles to give counseling {(A), (B)}.

132. C: The italicized phrase is an example of the future perfect tense of the verb. Tense is one grammatical category. Other grammatical categories include (but are not limited to) person (A), that is, first person = I/we/us; second person = you; third person = he, she, it, them. Another is case (B), that is, nominative/subjective, where a noun is the subject, accusative/objective where a noun is the object, or possessive/genitive indicating possession, for example, "*John's* hat". And the last, here is number (D), for example, singular (e.g., "hat") or plural (e.g., "hats").